The Sexual and Political Anorexia
of
the Black Woman

ALSO BY JULIA HARE

How to Find and Keep a BMW (Black Man Working)

And in collaboration with Nathan Hare (author of The Black Anglo Saxons):

The Black Agenda

Crisis in Black Sexual Politics

The Endangered Black Family

The Miseducation of the Black Child

Bringing the Black Boy to Manhood: The Passage

Fire on Mount Zion: An Account of the Black Holocaust of 1921 in Tulsa ("Black Wall Street"),
As told by Mabel Little

THE SEXUAL AND POLITICAL ANOREXIA OF THE BLACK WOMAN

By

Julia Hare

Foreword
By
Nathan Hare

Black Think Tank Books

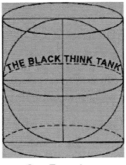

San Francisco

THE SEXUAL AND POLITICAL ANOREXIA OF THE BLACK WOMAN

First Edition
First Printing 2008

ISBN: ISBN.0-9817999-090000

Published by
BLACK THINK TANK BOOKS
1801 Bush Street, Suite 118
San Francisco, CA 94109
www.blackthinktank.com

Cover design by Lani Hunt
Front cover art by Phebe Durand, Printed in the U.S.A.
Back cover art by Vogue Art Distributors, A Division of Posterville, Inc.

Printed in the United States of America

To my sisters, the mothers of the universe

ABOUT THE AUTHOR

Dr. Julia Hare, was chosen by *Ebony* magazine as one of the one hundred most influential African-Americans, after she electrified Tavis Smiley's "State of the Black Union" conference carried "live on C-Span." *YouTube* video clips quickly chalked up more than a million hits on the internet as viewers passed her eloquent tidbits around the world. A gifted speaker, Dr. Hare is sought after nationally and internationally. She is a product of Tulsa's "Black Wall Street" where she has been inducted into the Booker T. Washington Hall of Fame. Dr. Julia Hare is the National Executive Director of the Black Think Tank, headquartered in San Francisco, where she currently lives with her husband, Dr. Nathan Hare.

DR JULIA HARE

CONTENTS

FOREWORD

By Nathan Hare[1]

When your woman tells you something to do, over a period of time you know what you have to do, but it was nevertheless a satisfaction to me when my wife asked me to write the foreword to her book on the pain and the glory of the black woman. Proceeding with caution, I hastened to read her manuscript in full, because I know my wife, and anybody who knows her knows that she is gifted with a very sharp tongue, which I have learned over the years is buttressed by a keen eye for uncovering any mischief in a man, not to mention her swift and surreptitious tactics of investigation.

So, armed with a secret aversion to the possibility of being seen as a traitor to my fellowman, I vowed to proceed with caution but with confidence accrued from years of collaboration with her in the cause of black male-female togetherness, in which I watched and learned in many ways her insider's awareness of the almost unbearable frustration and agony of the black woman. I also gained a deeper level of empathy with the black woman's historical hurts as "the backbone of the black family,"

---

[1]EDITOR'S NOTE: Author of *The Black Anglo Saxons* and founding publisher of *The Black Scholar*, Dr. Nathan Hare was the first coordinator of a black studies program in the United States.

when the black woman was sometimes going it alone and "going in the dark" with no man to stand beside her.

The black woman is weary now of being the backbone, but proud of it and at the same time secretly afraid that her strength will someday be the death of her relationship with her man; so that most of the time, when you see a strong black woman she is looking for a strong black man. And most strong black women will tell you they would give their right arm to have a strong black man to stand beside them.

Not surprisingly, we are being introduced here in this book not only to the black woman's pain and glory but also to a new way of looking at the black man and his connection to the pain of the black woman, as well as a new psychological malady, an epidemic the author labels "sexual anorexia," to which she adds the interesting corollary, "political anorexia," now rapidly emerging in a morally decadent world.

I can say only that I came away from a reading of this book imbued with an escalated awareness that to know the black woman fully you must walk in her shoes, so that as a black man writing a foreword to a book on black women, it is necessary to be both wary and brave. What can I as a black man say to black women who have had to deal with the white man's unparalleled wrath as well as the black male's misplaced rage in retaliation for the oppression of us all? Maybe it's a bit too much for a black man so much as to show his face, let alone open his mouth, but I decided to take the liberty to operate on the principle that if I am a part of the problem I should like also to be a part of the solution.

Maybe as men and women we can never really gain a full familiarity with one another's heartaches and disappointments. But being outsiders to the natural experiences and conditions of the other, the opposite sex (though we are locked together in the same race indelibly), we can come to know each other completely only by fusing our imaginations and our caring in creative new ways designed to ensure that our empathy and our bond will be unbroken. And it will be good for us to arm ourselves with the understanding that it is our very disagreements and the way we handle them – not our agreements – that will constitute the remedy for our hurts and the tenor and longevity of our lives together.

In any event it will always be necessary for us to understand that after all is said and done, in the end we are locked in this thing together, we are on the same side, and we all want the same thing: love and happiness.

Thus it is that black men, marching in atonement one million strong, will dare to demand a modicum of forgiveness from black women, if not a full understanding of the impact of oppression and its decimation of our devotion and our relentless sense of duty. Our women reply that we should stop crying on the black woman's shoulder and stiffen our backs and "man up" to break the chains of self-pity and a purposeless life, even if we cannot free the black woman and her children from the white man's deathly grasp.

"Give me just a little more time," the black man cries, but it is apparent from a reading of this book on "The Sexual and Political Anorexia of the Black Woman" that the black woman is "sick and tired of being sick and tired" -- and more and more the black woman will not wait.

PREFACE

By Julia Hare

Just before the outbreak of the AIDS epidemic in America, there arose on the sexual scene a little known emotional disorder, an affair of the heart that threatened the safety and the sanctimony of black women everywhere. We at the Black Think Tank were quick to discover this new malady in our clinical work, including the Kupenda (Swahili for "to love") black love therapy groups we were leading, and our torchlight studies in black male-female relationships.

Then, on the eve of troubling signs of black family decay in the 1970s, there appeared a curious syndrome we began to call "sexual anorexia" (loss of interest or appetite for romantic relationships, in a gut reaction to feelings of being unloved and unlovable). Soon this condition was noted by psychologists and psychiatrists in other races and quietly but quickly began to strike the black woman with the full force of an emotional tsunami.

One day in Seattle, I saw a wall high portrait of a solitary black woman hanging in the black student center on the campus of the University of Washington. Beneath it lay the caption, "Bearer of Pain," illuminated by slivers of sunlight shining through the window pointing the way to that painting and this book.

Julia Hare
San Francisco
May 1, 2008

Part I
SEXUAL ANOREXIA

Chapter 1

The Pain Guts and Glory of the Black Woman

Ever since the black woman was kidnapped and dragged to this country in chains and shackles -- starved, raped, impregnated at random, and sometimes thrown overboard, or otherwise died on board draconian slave ships crossing the turbulent Middle Passage -- she has found herself subjected to morbid experiences of squalor, depression, deprivation and plunder.

Death hung over her wind-battered head from the moment they took her out of Africa, her babies wrenched from her very womb and tossed overboard to unknown vultures of the dark ocean depths. Predatory men have raped her; killed her, impregnated her against her will.

From the moment they snatched her out of the motherland, heartache and dejection have hunted and haunted her night and day, day and night; and this quality of hurt has been compounded even more by daily karate chops of oppression, by her victimization, by domination and humiliation on top of historical hurts and sorrows for over four hundred years. And these were repeated in the course of her relentless experience of institutionalized prejudice and resistance from her lost days of chattel slavery, when she was sold away from her children or made to watch her children sold away from her, separated from her mates and other kindred and scattered around the globe, all over what is now a dispersed and disunited black Diaspora.

Forced at last to land on alien American shores, drenched and degraded in a strange environment, stripped of home and family, her pride and identity shattered and torn, she was auctioned and sold away from her children and her children from her. In a sense she stood in the naked condition of a brood sow, an captive breeder of slaves, often by her master, and for him and his progeny; and this is but a preview of the suffering she would endure over the centuries of her enslavement and oppression down to the present day, when government social workers will swoop in under the authority of the welfare department and take her children away in the service of protecting them when she is poor, or because she is poor, and deemed to have "too many children without a man" in a social condition in which the supply of males has been depleted.

Today the black woman remains the only female in this country who is not seen as a woman, who is denied her place on the pedestal of femininity while being allotted only the barest and most begrudging qualities of a sexual object, stigmatized by the wrath of mean white men who once sent their sons in chamber rooms and maids quarters to practice on the black woman in preparation for an ultimate consummation of marital relations with the white "ladies." Even today black women are not considered "trophy wives"; the only pedestal they are place on is three-inch high heeled platform Manolo Blahnik or Jimmy Choo shoes. This is just the tip of the iceberg that has brought on what I am calling the black woman's sexual anorexia (loss of appetite for sex and love relations) and political anorexia (the loss of interest and a turning away from their own political and psychological struggles) -- which we will take up in detail later.

Sexual Anorexia

Many recent events have escalated the agony and the magnitude of sexual anorexia in the black woman, impacting her wherever she goes in her personal and professional life where vicious stereotypes associated with her routine daily experiences have exacerbated the quality and severity of her suffering. When people stop and stare and sneak furtive glances, their stares may often represent no more than some random distraction; but to the black woman who must live with such humiliations daily, these furtive glances conjure up and rubberstamp the stereotypes by which the media (newspapers, television, books and magazines) incessantly bombard and pulverize her psyche. The effect in turn filters down into the schools and the minds of her children where it kindles misconceptions and conflicts sparking fights among unwary students.

Political Anorexia

By way of introduction, let us recall the issue involving the almost lily white Duke University lacrosse team that broke college rules to invite a stripper, a black coed from a historically black college, for their nighttime entertainment, no doubt acting out some gratification of the well-known sexual fancies found in the literature and the history of the races in this country, so spiced with "slave winches," concubines, Jezebels, street harlots and prostitutes.

Following the young stripper's accusations of rape, the media ran with the notion that she was some kind of a prostitute, while black women cringed in fear and silence before the cunning white male spin that the black strip dancer was a prostitute, a whore, something echoed by their female cohorts. Black women stood appalled; you could hear their dismay forever on their tongues wherever they came together, for they had already heard the cries of the now faded white feminist movement arguing that a "prostitute" could be raped as well as any woman.

The white male powers that be went on to acquit the affluent white lacrosse players under a shroud of silence conveniently announced in the media hurricane that surfaced when the Imus case broke. Don Imus, a high-rolling shock jock host of the popular MSNBC "Imus in the Morning," called a predominantly black female basketball team "nappy-headed ho's" -- after his executive producer had called them "hard core ho's" but escaped the burning bush. Another former associate of Don Imus blatantly opined: "the more I look at Rutgers they look exactly like the Toronto Raptors." Then the executive producer came back with a description of the NCAA championship game between Rutgers and Tennessee as "a Spike Lee thing" ("the Jigaboos vs. the Wannabes") and the rigmarole broke out in a media feeding frenzy of innuendos and insinuations assaulting the quality and pride of the black woman but by the time you read this book, Don Imus will be back on his show millions richer but effectively unscathed.

Behind the "Spike Lee joint," according to "Media Matters," lurked a *New York Times* article many years ago on Spike Lee's "School Daze" (in which the women of the iconic black college were "divided into two camps, the dark "Jigaboos' and the fair 'Wannabees' shown dissing each other as "pickanninies" "tar babies" and "high yella heifers)." In still another broadcast, according to a *Newsday* report, the executive producer had previously said "one of these days you're gonna see Venus and Serena Williams in Playboy," while somebody else in the studio added the brazen suggestion that they would have "a better shot at *National Geographic*."

The sensibilities of black women were already shaken to the quick when "Nappy headed ho's" came out of the mouth of a high-profiled public white man like Don Imus, for they had long been distressed by insults of this heartless sort. But equally as startling was the fact that black women did not storm the pearly gates of the Duke University campus, for fear of the adverse consequences, we all know black women do not suffer insults lightly. Where were the organized black women, the sorors -- the AKA's, the Deltas and the Zetas? Where were the likes of the National Black Business and Professional Women, the National Council for Black Women, or the National Coalition of 100 Black Women, The Links? Where were the missionary societies of the black churches?

Where were the members of the Congressional Black Caucus appointed to watch over us? Especially the black Congresswomen (we have no black female senators) who would later choose to support the white female opponent of the present and only black male senator running for president of the United States. None went straight down to the campus of Duke. They seem more inclined to step up for issues of their own political party than the issues of their own people who sent them to office, and in this they are like too many black women who are climbing up in whatever field: they forget about the sisters who haven't made it in life; and when they do step up they fear being knocked back to ground zero or knocked out altogether; but the only way that they can stop this is through the combined, organized and concerted efforts recognizing that if it happens to one today it can happen to another tomorrow, if not this evening.

Hillary Clinton went to Rutgers when the Imus smear was raging but never referred to Imus by name, and appeared to be more interested in turning the indiscretion of the lacrosse white male (one black) players into a white feminist issue, which the media was already doing; for instance, cut-lines in television footage would often read "gender and race," instead of "black women" or "the rape of a black woman." When other ethnic groups are victimized or standing up for a cause they're called and they call themselves just what they are: Asians, Hispanics or Native Americans, because they know they don't need black women to save them; they save themselves while black women save everybody but ourselves.

Whenever there is an issue in the news media affecting black women, many black women will get together to complain that there are almost no black female anchors or commentators. When newscasts do have black female commentators they are mainly on weekends, or in the "ghetto hour" when everybody else is sleeping, or on holidays, when the regular broadcasters have escaped work for higher purposes, and the news is generally what has already gone on during the week, over and over, in a secondhand replication of the weekday fare. Meanwhile we see women of all nationalities and races participating in high profile issues, many affecting black women but with black women missing in action or excluded from the dais. Not surprisingly many will deign to rationalize "oh, that's off limits to me – why should I be doing anything about that, why should I participate in that?" In effect they throw in the towel saying "this isn't for me" instead of "we're not represented here" and it's more imperative than ever that we begin to get involved; not as "women of color," not as "minority" women, not as "women," nor even African-American women, but as "black women." Whenever the issue is on white women, that's who's sitting there as the talking heads.

In the Duke and Imus events black women continued to listen while the media shepherded in black male civil rights leaders such as Jesse Jackson and Al Sharpton calling for Imus's firing. When you are discussing a critical issue such as black women on the media, representatives of that group, in this case black women, should be on every station talking; but the

Imus story was everywhere without them, on just about every station, twenty-four-seven.

The advertisers did finally pull Imus off the air for a while, but there are thousands of advertisers out there. If a station pulls the plug on a show host it does not mean they are necessarily finished for good, especially if they're popular and white, and even so there are usually hundreds more waiting in the wings to swoop down and carry on.

As I write, the word on the vine is stations are already looking at Imus, already booking him, and preparations are being made by some to bring him back, suggesting that Imus is merely waiting in some small radio station until the coast is clear again, then Honey, Imus will be back. Sisters, would a black man be given a microphone again after insulting a white woman who'd been violated by black men. By contrast, the fate of the black woman is likely to be uncertain; once a black woman reaches an upper niche and falls from her high place, it's virtually impossible for her to surface again, let alone return to the place where she had been on high.

Recall the halftime show at Super Bowl XXXVIII and the fallout from the exposure of one of Janet Jackson's breasts by the white crossover–to-black singer Justin Timberlake, the one who had hung out with black singers long enough to learn all their moves, how to walk that walk and talk that talk while catching their crotches rhythmically on cue. During the Super Bowl halftime entertainment the dynamic Janet-Justin duo hooted to the beat of "Rhythm Nation" and "Rock Your Body" as they went through hip-twisting hip hop gyrations with boodies and sexuality flying in the air. Finally, the singing reached a fatal line when Justin Timberlake crooned "I'm going to have you naked by the end of the show" and unceremoniously snatched off Janet's holster to reveal one naked breast. Janet was wearing jewelry underneath that gave the impression she'd had her nipples pierced, so the newspapers gave more ink and television gave it more coverage than the Super Bowl itself. These are the same self-righteous media outlets that claim to be weary of covering half-dressed Miss Americas and x-rated magazines exploding from the newsstands and coeds wearing thongs exposing cracks and "cleavage."

In an obsessively big-breasted culture commandeered by white males, it is nevertheless hard to see how one of Janet Jackson's breasts could so excite the public imagination. Politicians and critics all issued position papers condemning the show and threatening high hosannas over the scandalizing of one teeny black breast. Even Justin Timberlake, before he capitulated and went on to capitalize on his newfound masculine admiration and attention, had the gall to open his foul mouth and howl that the breast episode had offended his family. Sophisticated Europeans couldn't understand why all the fuss was being made about the exposure of one breast in America, a country long known to be obsessed with breasts in fanatical proportions. We do know that all the way back to plantation days, black men have been known to favor boodies while white men favored breasts (leading analysts to opine that it had some connection to the white man's historical experience of "nursing" from the breasts of black mammies).

Anyway, suits were filed against the FCC (Federal Communications Commission), and the incident threatened to cripple Janet Jackson's singing career while Justin Timberlake's career took off big-time, and Janet Jackson's stature was never the same again. Understandably, Janet soon fell into a fury of depression, gained weight and was out of sight and out of mind for a spell. Admittedly to his credit, Justin finally adopted a gentlemanly stance and conceded that America is tougher on "black and ethnic women." That was a white man saying that. Nothing at all ever seemed to happen to the streaker, who had flitted around the field unclothed, with only these words "Super Bowel" adorning his body against a background of television commercials advertising remedies for erectile dysfunctions, including one of a dog attacking a man's sexual problems. Meanwhile, offstage, Janet became a poster girl for a wave of false piety aimed at cleaning up Super Bowl and television entertainment for everybody and the ever elusive goal of public decency in America.

As the saying goes, when a man falls he can jump back up and brush his suit off and still have respect in his community, but a woman wears a scarlet letter. "When a woman falls off the curb, especially a black woman, she has to stay in the gutter. " Not long ago a black congresswoman from Georgia, Cynthia McKinney, had a confrontation with a Capitol Police Officer, a white male. How could that happen? According to news reports she refused to show her badge or identification on grounds that it was a place that persons like her go through almost daily. The white policeman chimed that McKinney had whacked him when he did not recognize that she was a congresswoman and ordered her to present identification, while the congresswoman accused the officer of "inappropriate touching" and "racial profiling" (implying a white female might have been treated differently).

Instead of sticking to the issues and actions that had erupted in the confrontation between the white guard and the black congresswoman, the news media and other critics focused on their assumption that Sister McKinney was channeling the Sixties-styled hairdo "freedom statement" (the afro or the "do") and the congresswoman had to fight to stay out of jail before eventually losing her job. Because she had been confronting this problem for eleven years whenever she wore her afro braids, she understandably wanted to know if she would have to change her hair style every time she entered the gate. According to the Honorable McKinney, the white guards were usually the ones that gored her the most on the days when she wore her braids.

When it was reported that the white guard put his hands on their black colleague's breast, black women in the Congressional Black Caucus did not fundamentally come to her aid. I can imagine the women of other races would have been up in arms if one of their nationally prominent sisters they had chosen to represent them had been the recipient of such nauseating treatment. But black women's lips were sealed; they didn't seem to understand that when a black woman is attacked in her racial physiognomy, it is an attack on the biology of all black women everywhere, especially in a world where they say we "all look alike."

Many other black women have been left, historically and presently, to swim with the sharks and brave the ocean alone. Star Jones was a black co-host of "The View" (hired and anchored by the legendary Barbara Walters); and, somewhat borderline obese, she was known to have weight issues and often was at odds with one of her white co-hosts. As usual for the media, Star Jones was the only black woman on the show, so when she hollered they let her go. The powers-that-be offered up the usual defenses and tried to say she was let go because of her ratings, but she maintained that it wasn't true. Some said she was fired because she had a "great big wedding" and thought everybody should donate a fee to snap a picture or get attention or even to be involved in the matrimonial swim. It was rumored she also had had her stomach stapled, because she thought she was too plump. They kept on a white woman who was plumper than her, the plumpest member of the cast. Even some black women rationalized that "Star Jones will get another high profile job," and "anyway, she's an attorney and can make a living." For some it was as if they clapped their hands. The pain was all Star Jones's. Like many women, she "wanted to be Cinderella for one brief, shining moment."

"I did….I wanted the white dress. I wanted the 926 bridesmaids. I wanted it all." Star Jones even admitted to "Good Morning America" that she'd gained seventy-five pounds then lost 150 "all in front of the world." Black women mumbled quietly in dark but failed to step up to the plate. While media hounds and the rumors and gossip hammered one of their own, they lost no rest.

Dorothy Dandridge almost made it to the top of the pedestal. Strikingly beautiful, she broke attendance records in Hollywood clubs and was one of the first black women to receive an Academy Award nomination. Nevertheless, it was said "she constantly battled insecurities about her looks and her talent and such anxiety often left her feeling physically ill before, during or after a performance." She had a hard time all of her life, from childhood on up, when she was allegedly abused by one of her mother's lovers; but Dandridge was brought down in the end by the demons of racism.

With all of her acclaim, Hollywood never gave her her due; they locked her in racial stereotypes of the era and restricted her to "lusty" and "tragic" character roles that seemed to play out in her off-screen marital life. Today she has a star on the Hollywood Walk of Fame, but in real life her story ends with another unhappy marriage, this time to a white man who abused her physically, even while he took her to the cleaners and left her broke from financing his failing business dealings. After the two-year marriage ended in divorce, Dandridge tried a comeback that failed. Then she was found in a hotel room dead of an overdose of prescription drugs for depression.

In a way, Ms. Dandridge was the prototype of the "domestic servant" and the "trampy seductress" roles that continue to plague black female stars in the present day. Halle Berry had done some fine acting in other films but received the Academy Award for her role as a single mother working as a low life in a 24 hour diner and took up with a trailer trash sheriff who had arrested and executed her husband and taken her as a lover. No less than Butterfly McQueen (who rationalized "she'd rather play a maid than be one any day"), Halle Berry got an award for the black female Jezebel stereotype.

****

After almost five centuries of the holocaust of her enslavement, long before shock jock Don Imus came on the scene, black women have been locked out of the higher echelons of beauty and femininity. The standard of beauty presented to her and the world remains blue eyes and blonde hair, but even when a black woman fakes it with peroxide, blue contact lenses and Miss Clairol, she knows when she looks in the mirror to remove her makeup at the end of the day that it was all a façade. Yet, in reality the black woman is subject to be raped by every nationality of males, physically and mentally, including her own, who is unable to save her from the rest. Through the many dark nights of plantation life gone by, and often in the daylight hours of today's megalopolises, the black man has been forced to watch the black woman violated. The black woman in turn has had to see the black man lynched for his alleged seduction of the white man's woman. Then, in a convolution of reason, too many black men still turn to the white woman to "get back at the white man." How pray tell can you get back at the man who has abused your women by loving his?

Today the black woman is compelled to watch the political and economic lynching of the black male, something akin to "hi tech lynching." Yet she knows that whatever impacts upon the black man affects the black woman also, just as whatever affects the black woman affects the black man: whether incarcerated in prison cages, blocked and all but eliminated from the labor force, or subdued by political impotence and emasculation. It is getting so bad that some black women have been heard to ask if they are now being forced to face the question, "do we have to become the new black men of the black community?" Or "is the black man becoming the new black woman?" What starts as a topic of conversation in beauty shops and conference seminars and Q and A's eventually emerges as a quasi-ideal, where more and more men are deserting their families and giving up on marrying at all, opting to seek out lonely women, sometimes considerably older, who can take care of them in unwedded splendor, or some are even slipping into the down-low.

But will it work? Is it possible for a race to be psychologically and sociologically viable without a patriarch in a patriarchal land? You used to could drive through the black community and see a lot of pretty women and a lot of working men; now you drive through the black community and see a lot of working women and a lot of pretty men, earrings and all.

So it should not be surprising that black male-female discussions more and more are breaking down in wars of misplaced rage. Solid solutions have been thrown aside and forfeited in quixotic quests for personal and gender revenge. Some women are weary now and sometimes giving up the fight altogether and sending the children of broken relationships to live with their "baby daddies" and their brand-new wives and children. Just as men have tended to have visitation rights when the children are with their mother, women now have visiting rights when the children are with their father. Some sistas go over to irk the new wife, wearing a plastic smile, legs crossed, dressed down to the nines in high heel shoes, in order to hang out in the new wife's home on visitation days to sit and smile and watch the new wife cleaning and sweating and cooking for the stepchildren she had never bargained for when she stole the affections of the sista's man after sneaking around with him. The wife whose husband was stolen delights in sneaking snide glances at the new wife's distress and embarrassment while admonishing her own children to "be nice to your step mommy" as she herself stands up and adopts an air of majesty while slowly taking her leave.

There was once a man in one of the Bible Belt states who had a loving wife and six children, replete with a white picket fence and a dog, before he met a younger woman and took the notion to leave his wife. To his surprise, the disheartened wife took all six children and left them with his new wife, who soon fled the waiting clutches of a dismal life. When a woman is going it alone or even when she's widowed, she retains the same desires as a married woman. She wants a man, a mate or husband to love her and herself alone; but if she so much as takes her children to the park she runs the risk of subjection to an inward rage seeing other men doing for their women what she feels her man should be doing for her. The same thing goes for the mall, the church, or the Sunday School for that matter. If she has sons she has to take to athletic activities her difficulties are doubled when she is sitting surrounded by white males or otherwise unavailable men opening car doors for their women and simultaneously helping with the children, sometimes with a child from a new mate's previous marriage riding papoose-style on his back. You can see how easy it is for the sister's spirit to crumble and her heart to break.

Day by day the black woman sees the white man on soap operas, television and movie dramas, in restaurants and public places, pulling out chairs and showering terms of endearment on their woman while constantly making the largely untenable claim that she is beautiful – questionable at least in the jaundiced eyes of the forlorn black woman looking on, the one compelled to look on in unrequited longing and disaffection, because she is unaccustomed to hearing that kind of talk from men in her own condition of poverty, brutality and blues, where men too often sing and say demeaning words: "You looking as ugly as a buzzard, woman," he might joke in hearty laughter and insensitivity, " you look like seven miles of bad road." "I'm going to Chicago, sorry but I can't take you, cause there ain't nothing in Chicago that a monkey-face woman can do," the black man sings in ill-mannered self-satisfaction.

Today, in the adolescent culture of hip hop music, this degradation of the woman a man's supposed to love has become an art form, set to riveting rhythm and harsh but captivating tones of alienation and rejection. As early as elementary school, black girls are indoctrinated with white storybook characters such as Snow White -- and the little black girls will raise their hands in hopes of being accepted and chosen as Snow White in school closing plays.

This is not quite as hurting to the boys at that stage yet because white males are not so much held up to them as standards of beauty; only the epitome of power and social potency. Black girls want to be as beautiful as society says the white girls are. Snow White and Cinderella, Fun with Dick and Jane, Goldilocks, pretty girls all in a row, these aren't black. Where a school is black, textbooks ought to be black. Asians have their own books, whites have their own books, blacks should have their own books; then, we could teach the history and the standards of beauty in our children's image, perhaps also giving our own take on little white lies and cherry trees and the discovery of America and the brave new world.

As things now stand, the black woman continues to be presented as a breeder of dysfunctional children in a society that clamps an anchor on her and her children and her mate. Stripped of the socialization and sometimes custody and contact with her children, she may be put in jail if she attempts to discipline them, and if she doesn't she may later have to watch them incarcerated. At every stage of the life cycle and at each and every turning point, she is more apt to have her children taken away from her than any other woman for little more than the consequences of living in poverty; impoverished, she stands to be punished again for being poor. Meanwhile the dysfunctional children of powerful people, from the president of the United States on down, are not taken away from them, although we see them on the evening news ---- the dysfunctional children of the high and the mighty -- stealing their doctors' prescription pads, sneaking in and out of rehab, getting into secret murders, yet going on to Ivy League colleges instead of jail. We see Hollywood stars and the rich and the famous whisking their children off to rehab programs or leaving them in the care of the governess, the maid and the nannies and whatever without sin, or any clear sense of shame.

Yet racial matters and the color complex are constantly fostered by Hollywood and the media in every way. When the film industry gives awards to black people, the black awards are almost always in synch with their stereotypes of black people. When Jennifer Hudson won the academy award in "Dream Girls," many black women whispered, "aren't you happy that a plump black woman got the award, but also Jennifer played a downtrodden and rejected black woman in her role.

When Vanessa Williams was set to be the first black Miss America in the history of the United States, the media dug up stuff on her days of youthful dalliance and dethroned her. They went snooping and sniffing until they found something they could use. They came up with suggestive risqué pictures from a porno magazine and defrocked her for that; not for her talents or her looks. Happily, her runner-up was of darker hue, but they gave her little attention and she quickly disappeared from the radar screen and then was seen no more. Sadly nobody knows her name now, or talks about her anymore, while Vanessa continues to sing, dance, act and marry at the top of the mart. The white world wishes not to see the black woman's beauty; it goes against their definition of beauty, which is light, white and pallid of skin, despite the fact that we all know that when it's black it doesn't crack.

Condoleezza Rice was the first black woman U.S. Secretary of State. A former professor of linguistics and a provost of Stanford University, Ms. Rice is fluent in several languages, and we see her on the news negotiating with heads of state in the middle of our wars. Regardless of her politics, Condoleezza is not celebrated for anything positive, but if she were a white woman, with the same facial features she has now, the same hair style, the choice of clothing, she would be praised to high heaven, or critics would elect to fall silent on her faults. Instead she's often speculatively linked to the president as his paramour, with rumors and conjectures of a purported romance threatening the president's family with divorce, and the tabloids burn with a towering inferno of innuendo and gossip. With the black woman, there may not be glory in pain but there is pain in her glory.

Some of the most popular black women in this country, whether they're athletes, mayors, astronauts, radio announcers, television talk show hosts or whatnot, at the end of the day they can always tell each other about the aggravation and racism they face, and they will tell you they believe it is because they are black. When the white woman is kidnapped – and of course this is a terrible thing for anyone – the story is prone to run forever on the news: the Aruba situation ran for almost two years and continues to crop up; there's also "the runaway bride" (black women have been running away for years). Chandra Levy seemed forever in the news when her death followed an alleged affair with a congressman; not to mention the late Anna Niccole Smith, a young woman with big breasts married to a wealthy octogenarian, with several men stepping up to claim parentage of her newborn baby, is still alluded to in the news like she was some kind of a queen.

Black women go missing almost daily all over the nation but get little coverage except on cop shows and occasional forensic and investigative reports. When white babies are missing, the "Amber Alert" goes up immediately, but when black babies disappear black women are left to face the despair and emotional devastation with only their closest relations. Maybe we should have a "Tamika Alert" for black women; then, maybe they can break free of the shackles of political anorexia.

Political Pain

When politics work against the black woman, her family and children are caught up in the quality of her hurt, and there is pain in the family. Whether she is successful (going up the social ladder) or going down, the political pain comes down on the black woman who is unable to rear and nurture her children or find and keep a good enough husband, a father for her children, while life all around her is falling apart.

What's falling apart? Even when there is food on the table, the rearing of her children may be weakened and obstructed for the low income mother who has been steadily losing the authority to discipline her children ever since white politicians and advocates of ultra-permissive childrearing, which is more amenable to the middle class condition, decided that discipline was to be outlawed as punitive although black women see their discipline as love. Without discipline, without a helpmeet, the task of keeping her children out of jail falls into the lap of the black woman. Years ago, before integration and mass urbanization, when black women controlled the care and comfort of their own families better, they would take the time to teach them that you will be watched more than anybody else in this society. They had to teach their boys that around whites you have to exhibit a special politeness or you are going to jail. Too bad that warning wasn't imparted sufficiently to Emmitt Till, who as a fourteen year old Chicagoan was on a visit back home to Mississippi and was lynched and thrown into the river after he whistled at a grownup white female store clerk while trying to impress his adolescent Mississippi buddies.

When I was growing up near "Black Wall Street" in Tulsa, Oklahoma, I learned that one of the worst race riots in American history had taken place there in1921. My father used to tell me how a young black man had gotten on an elevator with a young white woman and the white woman jumped off the elevator and claimed the black man had stepped on her toe. Soon a riotous mob of white men moved slowly but ominously toward the black community looking for the black man who had stepped on a white woman's toe. That was the kind of thing that made black people teach their sons to stay out of elevators for fear of some chance encounter with a white woman that might land them in jail or get them killed. Black boys were admonished never to go over to the white part of town or glance at a white woman anywhere. They were teaching their sons how to stay alive. Even today the black woman has to spend a lot of her time preparing and indoctrinating her children against the psychosocial hassles and horrors of race that white mothers and their children within socioeconomic serenity of the suburbs and the protective safety net so often provided by the police and the courts.

The black woman is more likely to lose her mate than anybody else, white or black male or female, due to the high unemployment, incarceration and underemployment of the black males. Accordingly, she suffers a shortage of BMW's (Black Men Working), and she is too often compelled to live with the pain of having her children taken away from her, by social workers in the ambiguous child abuse and child custody system, to be placed by the courts in alien foster homes and subjected to all the institutional devices now existing to take the place of the family in a society in which underprivileged parents are steadily losing the authority to rear and discipline their children. Meanwhile, we see white society sending people out from hospices to help the ill, along with maids and nannies to train affluent children. We send the firefighters out when there is a fire. We send policemen out when there is a homicide. We could likewise send people out to teach and help the single mother parent.

The black woman suffers for herself and her family. If the husband leaves and gets with someone else -- which he often does -- the black woman is confronted with all the issues of raising her children: her man coming in and out of her house to pick up the kids and see who's there, trying to find some sign of some other man, titillating her now and then to see if the flame is still burning, blocking out other men who will get the impression he's still got himself in the game and will be in a huff if anybody else, some other man, keeps on coming around. And the worst pain of all is when her children grow up and wonder if she drove their father away, and sometimes become a somewhat estranged from her, instead of taking their rage out on the father, the one who went away, the one who deserted them.

History of Struggle

Bearer of Pain

We know black women can boast of a long proud history of fighting oppression, of coping with powerlessness and standing against their political pain. The black woman is inscribed in an undeniable history as "the backbone of the black family," the "bearer of pain," an unrequited legacy of going the last mile, "reaching for the sky," "doing it to death," "loving too long to stop now," fighting for her family and making ends meet, many times suffering but always fighting back and reaching landings and standing beside and sometimes in front of her man.

Ida B. Wells

Ida B. Wells spent a lifetime trying to end the long vicious lynching, most notably of black men. She was to lynching what Rosa Parks was to segregation. Publishing and advocating against lynching, she rallied against the lynching of black men and almost single-handedly forced the reluctant government to step in, so that the lynching of black men after 1921 (also by chance the year of the bombing of "Black Wall Street") was never quite the same again. Although an ardent activist in the suffragist movement, she exposed as myth the rationale that white men were lynching black men for the "rape of white women" instead of the white man's own hidden sexual fears and his dogged opposition to black economic progress, his claims of black inferiority, and fears in reaction to the undying threat of the rise of black men.

General Tubman

We could call the names of hordes but need only mention one, Harriett Tubman (Araminta Ross), who was one of eleven children born into slavery but made a vow to resist when she saw her master punishing another slave by picking up a piece of iron and throwing it at him but missed and hit Harriett, leaving her to suffer a permanent scar and seizures for as long as she lived. Rather than slipping into political anorexia, Harriett Tubman joined the Underground Railroad and served as a nurse, also as a cook and a spy, on the side of the Union Army in the Civil War before she made history as the conductor of the Underground Railroad. She returned many times, fearlessly, to the South to rescue slaves; and, once she had gained her own freedom, ushered an estimated three hundred slaves out of slavery and said she "could have freed thousands more, but they didn't know that they were slaves." It has been related that some of the brothers among those freed had a mind to turn around and head back, but General Tubman would pull out her gun and tell them to keep on moving or, "I'll shoot you myself." She reputedly once said that in all her work with the Underground Railroad, she never lost a passenger and never ran a train off the track. Could Amtrak claim that?

Black female freedom fighters are also legion in modern times, though most remain in obscurity, unknown and unsung: Fannie Lou Hamer, Ada Lois Sipuel Fisher, Kathleen Cleaver, Angela Davis, Queen Mother Moore, Shirley Graham DuBois, Little Rock's Daisy Bates, Gloria Richardson. Assatur Sakur, *ad infinitum*, proving a black woman doesn't have to submit to sexual and political anorexia.

Queen Mother Moore

Audley Moore, nicknamed Queen Mother Moore, was a strong black freedom fighter for most of her life and a mentor to many young men and leaders, including Malcolm X, Max Stanford and Nathan Hare in the Black Power movement of the late 1960s. Queen Mother fought for the worldwide unity of Africans in America and elsewhere and almost single-handedly revived and rekindled the demand for black reparations.

Lady Day

The legendary blues singer, Billy Holiday, better known as "Lady Day," was known to resist incessantly the exploitation of black musicians. Lady Day never succumbed to political anorexia and seldom failed to tell her listeners how the music industry was trying to use her labor and talents for pennies: "Papa may have, mama may have, but God bless the child that's got his own."

Mothers and Great Grandmothers

It's said if you educate a woman you educate a race, but how quickly we forget what our mothers and our grandmothers told us when they boasted how they had gone as far as the eighth grade in school and would have gone farther if they'd had the chance. They'd ramble on about the fact that they "may not have been to no college, ain't swallowed no grammar or eaten no 'rithmetic, ain't been in no Who's Who, but I know What's What."

Got to Give it Up

Yet political powerlessness and the loss of appetite for things political (a political disdain), is part and parcel of too many of the black woman's feelings of resentment, fury and rage, of despair and hopelessness. The ultimate source of her political anorexia is of course the white dominated political world that the white slave masters and slave mistresses made. Today, the black woman is impelled to sit and talk and complain and grumble, to nitpick and whine, to vent more than to act, only to find that in the end, when all is said and done, nobody much wants to share her pain.

Though racial oppression looms as the original and most continual generator of the black woman's alienation, it is not the only source (whether within or without) of undeniable and enduring symptoms of political anorexia today. Many traditional black churches do not allow black women to preach or even to go up and stand at the pulpit, except to read announcements or lift an offering, prepare the Lord's Supper, or the pastor's upcoming anniversary, or the Pastor's Guild. She keeps the church finances moving, the organization going, and the preacher fed; the black church could not function without black women, it could not run; and yet she allows the men to be the preacher, and some sisters go so far as to say they would not belong to a church with a female preacher. So while there are a million black men in jail waiting for justice, there are a million women in church waiting for Jesus.

As smart as church sisters are, they should know that the pastor serves at their behest, he is their employee. Tell the preacher what you want things to be, and if he doesn't agree, tell him to take his tithing envelopes, pack his robes, and take his clerical collar and go. Sometimes we forget there is more than one church in town, and sometimes somebody's got to go. If the preacher refuses to leave tell him like Patti LaBelle said in the song: "you can call me crazy, you can call me stupid, but call me gone."

Chapter 2

The Fight for Love and Glory

The Scorned Woman

In every income level or race or nationality lurks someone known as a scorned woman. We all know one, but today they are prone to exhibit a tiny but notable difference: one type prefers to handle her emotional bruises privately while the other goes public. You may recall the rampant though unverifiable rumors surrounding Cicely Tyson and her undying love and loyalty for Miles Davis in the face of his unmitigated gall to take her love for granted and proceed with his admitted meanderings and posturing in public places. But in another time and place, it was the popular British talk show host David Frost who brushed off the diva Diahann Carroll, the toast of black and white America. The diva camouflaged her scorn with Fashion Fair makeup but never could quite cold-cream it away from public view after Frost not only neglected to marry her but also distanced himself in the media. While Frost remained the toast of London, Diahann never quite made it back, repeatedly marrying other suitors (including songbird Vic Damone and a promising *Jet* magazine editor, young enough to be her son, who left his wife and three children for the bright lights and Diahann Caroll but picked up an addiction to drugs until one night he drove off a California mountain to an untimely death).

In white celebrity high class social circles Marilyn Monroe could have been toast, but Jackie O didn't even bend over to turn on the oven, feeling that to come forward with such a thing would plummet her into the middle of a public scandal while elevating the mistress to her secret delight. Hillary Clinton didn't divorce President Clinton; her agenda was bigger than Bill and a mistress.

Just about any woman who is to the manor born in white society's upper strata can sit back and take her lumps in style, but the black woman trapped in modest means may have to resort to grassroots "survival techniques," dealing with her transgressors and baby daddies one on one. The black woman knows the higher she goes up the social ladder too few black men will be there waiting for her, so she may just have to survive and say to Hell with the public. If she loses out altogether and her man goes away, she may have to hang her head in silence because she doesn't want to leave the house on the hill and return to the poverty and decadence of the inner city. If she's truly wise she doesn't even mention it to too many friends -- and the media is out of the question. Many black middle class women caught in these "playing" relationships will seal their lips when these personal indiscretions visit them. They have learned down through the generations that you can do almost anything to handle a situation so long as it is done with considerable discretion. There's no such thing as confiding your heart-on-the-sleeve love problems and indiscretions to your snooty girlfriends; leave that to the class that gets on the Jerry Springer show.

I remember a high profile black mega-minister, who was swimming in faith-based money, and who gained a tarnished reputation in a sizeable Northeastern city for exclusively dating white women and flaunting a brazen and particular obsession with blondes. His church flaunted "diversity," which attracted tithing and single white women, and it was soon obvious to many that this brother needed the same psychiatric couch that Michael Jackson is presumed to have used to cope with allegations of a reputed paranormal curiosity for little white boys. As for the high profile preacher, many sisters concluded that this seemingly intelligent black clergyman's mania for white women was as pathological and addictive as Rush Limbough's oxycotin. Being long estranged but not divorced from his black wife and children, Brother Minister had the entire field of lonely and alluring black females crowding the front row pew in short skirts and crossed legs waiting for him to date without commitment or marriage. It didn't matter to him what color they were, so long as they didn't look like him or his mother. He didn't date black skin women. I mean this brother could have been a perfect Freudian study for contemporary shrinks who contemplate and ponder the psychic trauma of oppressed black males addicted to the white oppressor's women while appearing to be allergic to women of their own melanin heritage. Due to the high amount of melanin in this brother's DNA, many black women concluded that his attitude was connected to multiple experiences of rejection by girls when he was growing up.

Many of the elderly black pastors and politicians who had made this brother what he was could not understand the odd aversion he displayed for so much as speaking to black people. For a while he blamed this on a hearing problem (presumably he could hear whites but couldn't hear blacks), proving that ignorance is often present among the most intelligent. If you can't hear, but you can see, you speak to anything that moves, but you sho' go'n speak to anything you see.

I recognize that some men of the cloth are sent and some *went* to the ministry and that pastors are frequently looking for some committee or commission to sit on in order to be the voice of the black community. But like the best of comedians and court jesters, the most pompous and self-anointed men of the cloth must have someone to play off of; and in the case of Brother Minister, it was usually black women. Not surprisingly, almost anytime two or more black women gathered for a talkfest, you could hear them whisper their disdain for him and for whatever woman (or women) he was currently seeing. Yet when he deigned to drop into predominantly black gatherings, these same black women who had just referred to him as everything but a child of God would all at once fall silent and even grovel at his feet, with or without the presence of cameras (when they were likely going to be ignored by him). Otherwise they were merely destined to watch him mete out ecclesiastical privileges and favors to white women of the church, while few black women got no more than a finger-licking of the frosting on the cake; and then only if the cake was chocolate. Sisters who were able to keep a keen eye out for stupidity usually ignored him, while the *wannabes*, the *neverwases* and the *nevertobes* stood around slobbering and clamoring for so much as a solitary nod from him.

When Brother Minister decided to run for political office, he took the advice of a Madison Avenue public relations flack and tried his hand at dating a black woman for a change. He remembered how sisters had passed out voting materials for him in the past, fried fish dinners and chicken dinners for fundraisers, and manned booths and telephone banks. Some even had carpools to help get out the vote; even when it was raining the cars would loop around the block. Yet in the end the black woman he decided to date was the closest thing he could get to *not* being black, what with her mixed heritage and, even more than Mariah Carey, could easily be mistaken for another nationality.

At first the sister he decided to date was treated in the sisterhood like Cinderella when the Fairy God Mother dressed her for the palace ball. She was wined and dined and by some maligned for dating the married preacher. There were the cars, the furs, the national and international junkets, not to mention the bragging of her introduction into high society. She didn't know the headiness of dating the mega minister would soon come to an end. When the polls predicted a victory for him in his campaign, he reverted to his old habits.

After the victory speech she found it impossible to reach him on the phone, but word soon started leaking out about his new love affair with a white woman and the ghetto Cinderella went into sexual bulimia, flitting from one man to another like a butterfly, but having grown accustomed to the highlife she now wanted only men who were on or above his level; they could be black pink or green so long as they had position, power and big spending prowess. This scorned black sister that the minister took up with when he was running for office -- and ditched when he won -- decided to run for elected office in the same city herself. She was not a woman to go home and give herself a pity party. In order to pick herself up she decided she would run for office and throw her hat in the ring for a position almost as high profile as his. At this point, several newspapers in the town that loathed the arrogance of her former pastoral lover made the scorned lady well aware of what was going on. She had already met a few newspaper editors and publishers herself through this man. Knowing she had gone around with the preacher-politician, they came to interview her about him.

Whether the interview was premeditated or off the record remains unknown, but when the reporter came to interview her, she went after the minister she had loved and added all the fodder the reporter needed, forgetting her own collaboration in the pastor's past indiscretions. During their love affair, she had made out with cars, houses, condos and cash, prompting some people to call her a prostitute working suites instead of streets. However, even after castigating the clergyman in the press, our scorned woman continued to accept his largesse through campaign contributions and his ability to twist the arms of local unions to endorse her. Maybe she knew but didn't want to know his endorsements of her were more about him than her, but she didn't go home and pull the covers over her head like many women do; she refused to let one affair throw her off keel. After she won the election some women applauded her and even suggested she give seminars. She went on with her life and on to other men, the more the merrier, in her reactive political bulimia, a type of political anorexic that mimics nymphomania in the quest for sexual and political prowess.

The Status Seeker

Is there anyone who can't put a finger on a friend or a sister or someone in your female circle who is a status seeker, a social climber who wishes to pull herself "up" to escape her romantic/sexual loneliness for popularity and recognition? One who's desperate to consort with high profile people with social chic, known to have connections and political savoir-faire. Be careful of these people. Social climbers will do whatever it takes for recognition and prestige, sometimes making "Billary"-styled political tactics seem mild in the context of their latte and tea-driven social klatches, climbers of the "Status Seeker" variety become social addicts because they're living lives of quiet desperation in search of an illusion. Many have degrees, admiration and respect from their families but still feel empty in the hollow pit of their stomachs. They feel overlooked as they've never received acclaim or recognition from the pillars of the community.

Recently a sister we'll call Margie came to the beauty shop and sat down in a seat where the lady just ahead of her had left a highbrow magazine that catered to affluent women who shop at high-end boutiques and department stores. Thumbing through the magazine while waiting for the operator to put her in the shampoo chair, Margie saw an article reporting on the Social Register and telling who the latest additions were. What a waste of time. It is more difficult to get listed in a city's registry of the prominent or the to-the-manor born than it is to get into the Ft. Knox or the Pentagon, but this didn't deter this climber. She snooped around to see if a "black book" or "Social Register" existed in the black community, forgetting that other than membership lists of elite social clubs and sororities, you'd be hard-pressed to find a bona fide social register in the black community. Many black society matrons in the black community aren't even registered to vote.

It happens Margie's own family was an embarrassment to her. Her mother and father scrubbed floors, did janitorial work, and mortgaged their house to send her to college, but she put her whole life and false sense of self-importance up for sale to escape any reminder of her humble beginnings, frantically trying to re-invent herself so as to have no reminders of her past. Some get rid of old friends for fear they may ask about an old boyfriend, not wanting to be reminded of unforgotten lovers. Some climbers acquire new zip codes, when possible, in their clamor to escape to higher grounds of love and acceptance. They search for new addresses with names such as "Hills," "Woods," or "Gated Community."

In her quest for social and sexual mobility, a social climber can smell a cameraman and a newspaper society editor as soon as she arrives at a gala or festivity, all five senses charged and blaring to alert her to stay on her feet and follow the scent of the photographer and the head socialite. She has studied and poured through the society and gossip columns, proclaiming all the while that she never reads black newspapers or their columns carrying grapevine-level scuttlebutt on the black crème de la crème.

The Status Seeker is fastidious in her conversation and is up on the manners and vernacular of the "high muckety-mucks." She refers to her condo as a "suite" (inasmuch as a lot of affluent white socialites have suites in hotels to stay in and invite friends for dinner when they come to the city). One status seeker recently told me this was to lend an appearance of upward mobility. Having a suite in a hotel like the officers of the organization impresses those in the group to which she wishes to climb. Social climbers are known to spend money they don't have for things they don't need to impress people who are hardly aware of their existence. They operate on the theory that newly acquired mannerisms, new friends, male and female, will convince themselves and others that they have arrived.

Shirley P. was a professional woman, a good-hearted individual, good-natured but carried the baggage of a multiplicity of failed relationships with men in the past and now appeared to be rushing to break Elizabeth Taylor's failed marriage record. She was an astute and tenured college professor, well read, well traveled, but could not curtail or conceal her difficulty in attracting and staying with a man. During an informal counseling session, I asked her why all the breakups. She rationalized that some of the men were high school dropouts, or didn't read or had "worked the same blue collar job for 25 years" and never moved up. Her rationalization was: "These black men didn't want anything." Why, I asked, do you continue to seek out the same type men, knowing your expectations will not be met? If you always do what you always did you will always get what you always got.

The status seeker broke down in paroxysms of disenchantment and tales of lost and unrequited love. Describing herself as obese she opined that blue collar males might treat her like a queen because of her corporate position and would be quite proud to parade her title among their blue collar buddies. No one had told her that men do not so much seek title and position in their mates, and may even be threatened by these characteristics; men are more into sex and physical appearance, charm and personality in their choice of a mate. They might prefer other things as well, but if a choice has to be made, the appearance is highly likely to win out. Status Seekers are so busy trying to get the man and the status they may often neglect or give too little attention to their appearance.

Status seekers are most effective when they keep their eyes peeled and focused on that group they feel the need to social climb up into. One matron who climbed to where and what she thought she wanted, told me she always asked herself certain questions: "Are the women from the suites or the streets?" Are they too old to go braless or to have the front of their dress unbuttoned down to their navels? Have their breasts dropped down to the waist because they're braless? Have they reached an age when it's time to give up sleeveless clothing? Are they parading around in yesterday's mini skirts which will only catch a cold and not a man. Are women in the group over 20 wearing their stomachs out? Are the ladies in the group in which you wish to climb exposing thongs when they bend over? Are you blinded by the bling bling that should only be worn by rap artists?

The middle-aged status seeker told me if the answer to one or more of those questions was yes, she was not going up the ladder, she was going down the ladder into the ditch, right along with the pretentious pillars she had admired. One day she was invited to a rather snooty luncheon given by a claque of local used-to-be still wannabe's gathered in their Pradas, Stuart Weizmans, Chanels and a few wore Blahnik and Jimmy Choo stiletto heels. The room was filled with whispers about where each had purchased their diamond tennis bracelets and Rolex watches and what bling bling was purchased by what patrician sugar daddy in the community. There was so much wasted money reflected in their clothing one could think these sisters had secretly gotten a down payment on their black reparations. One woman walked in wearing a simple black pant suit, a white shirt, a straw-brimmed hat and some black pointed toed boots. She carried a small clutch purse (no visible designers initials) and simple hoop earrings (probably costume jewelry) and a small gold wedding band.

Many of the pillars of the community stared admiringly at this woman. Some of the more courageous moseyed up to her to introduce themselves and give her their business cards while they looked her up and down, wanting to know what kind of work she did. Many of the St. John wearers had committed cardinal no-no's; they wore several rings on each hand and other trappings of the "uniform of sorors who lunch" -- no imagination. Jeanette abhorred faddish trends but loved fashion and style. She instinctively knew designers create trends, unaware that the individual woman creates her own fashion.

They all thought they were dressed to the nines but everybody (including escorts and husbands) was admiring the mystery woman whose clothing, except her underwear, unknown to them, had come from thrift stores and consignment shops she owned. Male escorts and husbands could be seen sneaking furtive glances at her. Before long the women at the luncheon, the social climbers and some of their friends were shopping at and consigning their clothing to her boutique. She didn't climb to them, they climbed to her.

One of the first resorts of women reeling on the merry-go-round of sexual anorexia is to seek refuge in the social loop of those they think have made it. In compensation for their frustrated sexual outlets, such status seekers claw and thrash about for men in the "fish bowl" of black "high society." They have a need to be seen with the socially prominent of both genders, the power brokers and those most likely to be featured in gossip and "society" columns of the local newspaper. They believe there can be no meetings unless they are there to put in their two cents worth of flash and sash and dressing for success.

One seeker, hooked on meetings, luncheons and organizations, was begged by her husband and family to have dinner just once in a while at home with the family. "Those meetings were here before you got here," he cried, "and will be here when you're gone." But she would hear none of that; she was obsessed with the need to be in the social mix. She sought the attention of what she referred to as the "A-list" in her community, people consisting of politicians, proprietors, silk stocking church pastors, attorneys, shrinks, M.D.'s, or the wives of such, and others who are practically household names in the community's "upper crust" or "society." If she could be seen with and accepted by the socially prominent, the door would open for her to get back at the black males who contributed to her sexual anorexia by putting themselves off limits to her. Sometimes she would boast to close confidants, "I'll show them I'm trophy material -- I can get any man I want." Denial didn't solve her problems. She was seldom seen with anybody in town, because the men in her life, according to her excuses, were always away consulting, or somewhere else preaching, speaking or attending board meetings in other sections of the country.

People in the social circles into which she wished to climb were well aware that men had heard rumors of her snobbish disposition, so she set out to replace her frustrated sexual aspirations with social analgesics and other means of sublimation (a defense mechanism in which you put your time and effort into more reachable and hopefully accessible pursuits). She took an oath with herself to make it into the who's who of the community while at the same time tweaking the indignation of the men who turned their backs on her and the women who snatched them by the pants and ran.

Sliding up the societal ladder is more socially acceptable and more attainable to the woman who has grown accustomed to rejection and, in her rejection, turned to the sour grapes of sexual anorexia. She will often be overheard to say she doesn't want a man but looks for her emotional salvation in a multiplicity of men, going for the fleeting and transitory one night stands and sleeping with men who aren't committed to long-term mating and dating relationships.

I was once invited to keynote a women's conference in a Midwestern city. The audience consisted of women of all persuasions, ethnicities and ages. A black woman slipped me a note inviting me to meet privately with a caucus of black women to "get down" and discuss some "sisters only issues." The usual question of the successful black woman syndrome was the first item on the table. Questions ranged from why the more education and material trappings a black woman has the harder it is to find and keep a BMW (Black Man Working)? Why are the few marriageable black men already married or scouting the terrain in search of the over abundant supply of women? One of the more reserved, pensive and almost shy sisters wanted to know "why we can't treat the brothers as they treat us: one night stands and week-end getaways to relieve our stress through sex. She told how she was "forced" to show up at high profile social events and try to be seen with popular women who always had the pick of the black male litter. Her solution was to become a social predator and if all else failed she could still always fight for love and glory.

The Social Nymph

Why are so many black women -- faced with an abundance of black men always at the ready for sex -- nevertheless suffering "sexual anorexia," the loss or lack of an appetite for full-fledged involvement in sexual relationships? Unlike the simple sexual anorexic, who is turned off from the virtual horde of males, the pseudo-maniacal anorexic woman gets turned off quickly in her encounters with one man but wastes no time moving on to another. The more the pseudo maniacal anorexic disdains to make the struggle or wage a full commitment to any one man, the more she becomes obsessed with dashing from man to man. In compensation, she settles for secondary gain and anything she can get out of a man in terms of money, jewelry, exotic trips, and invitations to the A list events. Women in this category tend to choose the man for what they can get, often the same man they would not look at if he worked an average job. Don't even mention not working at all. Save that for pimps and whores. With the social nymph, the pleasure is all hers; or so it would appear.

Seeing the anorexic nymph going from high level man to man, other women will stand by and applaud her, thinking they know what it's all about. Not so! Often the pseudo anorexic nymphomaniac is a bruised and aching woman, not just by one man but numerous men. In every income level, in spite of race, national origin, age or positioning in society there lurks the anorexic nymph, a scorned woman. Skin color, pimples or national origin of the man is no deterrent to the pseudo nymph, as long as she gets what she wants. She will lead the diatribe and the chorus if a black man even looks in a slanted direction at a white woman.

While political issues are stabbing local and national black communities, killing our schools, our relationships, our existence and our ability to survive, black women are slipping into political anorexia: a turnoff from recognizing, battling and solving political issues. Both actions, sexual and political, accumulate from deeply simmering and unresolved conflicts with the opposite sex and our continuous political meanderings. In a sense it is no wonder some sisters disdain and refuse involvement in the political and sexual arenas, weary now of a bruised and aching heart – assaulted in the bosom of her beauty, her body itself, the color of her face, the soul of her being.

Chapter 3

The Politics of Black Skin and Hair

When bestselling public intellectual Michael Dyson invited me to his national radio show, I knew his topics were always politically charged, but I was not prepared for what would happen that day. We'd worked on panels together, including Tavis Smiley's CN N Broadcast of The State of the Black Family, State of the Black Race and the State of just about everything plaguing black folk, and crossed paths at the Congressional Black Caucus Conclave in Boston as well as *Essence* Magazine's Annual Empowerment Seminars in New York and New Orleans. So when the show's producer called to say the show would focus on the status and politics of something concerning urban America, I wondered what we would talk about now. Hadn't we covered every menace to black folk? Not quite! After the usual introductions, Michael told the listeners he couldn't resist reading a rather disturbing email from a "sister." Her letter said she hated being a black woman. She described her skin as "jet black" and said her artistic Afro hair style was shameful to her family, church and light-skinned girl friends. She ran down all the reasons she hated being a black woman: her black skin color was killing her; she couldn't get jobs that under-qualified white women were getting, and she hated raising a black son; she had finally confessed to the reasons for her "depression and distressing disgust with everything. "

The dark-complected woman's comments attracted a quick volley of calls to the station from listeners who were taken aback and appalled that a black woman would publicly express such hatred of being a dark-skinned woman. It was not surprising that the sisters hit the phone lines but that they personally and openly identified with her plight. Black women have long harbored a crushing skin color and hair hang-up, almost to the day black folk were kidnapped from Africa and planted in America.

In Africa, before the invasion and colonization of the continent, it had seemed aristocratic for a woman to have that elegant wooly crown protecting the head from heat strokes, sun burns, and skin and scalp disorders. Plus you didn't have to expend too much energy on maintenance. The vogue, the custom, was *au naturalle*. When a black woman looked in the mirror, she enjoyed a good look at her native good luck. Her brilliant jet black skin was worn with a stateliness that matched and spotlighted her strong melanin-enriched heritage.

Over the ensuing centuries, one of the harshest sources of hurt and cultural shock to the black woman has been the fickle definitions of beauty that negated and rejected her. Thus it was that radio shock jock Don Imus put his foot in his mouth when he described the stellar almost all-black Rutgers University women's basketball team as a bunch of "nappy-headed ho's," humiliating a handsome coterie of young black women whose mothers and grandmothers were dragged across rivers and oceans to slave for the likes of Imus and his women and to nurse and nanny the progeny of his race. A woman is basically valued or chosen as a mate, or as a "trophy wife," and placed on a pedestal based on the way she looks (with her beauty and consummate value defined by the powers- that-be and, in the case of the black woman, will wish to deny her her beauty if they have their way).

Meanwhile, according to psychoanalysts, if there is a psychological component to the sexual encounter between the male and the female, it is that the female is the receiver of the male effort to release his sexual passion while the challenge of the female is the need to feel desired and desirable. It is at this point that the black woman confronts a special whammy, because unlike women of other ethnic groups, the black woman is rejected in her physical qualities, her corporeality, her physiognomy, the way she looks -- which conspires to strike the black woman in the heart of her feminine need to feel desired and desirable.

Plantation life and the raping of black women by white men particularly impacted this. When the master's black progeny, a light-skinned mulatto, was granted compensations (lighter chores, respite and retreat from the fields to the big house and the shade), the African slaves in time internalized and emulated the slave society's notions and definitions of beauty -- blonde hair, blue eyes and light skin as the subjugated blacks, including black women, assimilated to the world they knew and its definitions that diminished the black woman and her black beauty. Psychiatrist Franz Fanon, in *Studies in A dying Colonialism*, once described this reaction as "over-identification with the oppressor." According to Fanon, when the oppressed begins to feel too weak to do combat with their oppression, they turn upon themselves, squabbling, bickering and breaking out in fratricide (killing and shooting one another), much like we're doing in our crabs-in-the-barrel condition that cultivates in too many of us these days a disturbing secret desire to go to sleep at night and wake up white. Many kidnapped or abducted children and adults have been observed to identify with their captors, behavioral scientists say, and we have watched any number of high profile blacks such as in Michael Jackson, OJ. Simpson, Clarence Thomas and Koby Bryant – not necessarily in that order -- identifying so strongly with their masters they get to thinking they are white enough to step out of line or out of place (at which point their masters and their fans move quickly to disown them and you see the erring brothers slinking back to the black fold to save them from the rousing white wrath, only to scamper back into the white obsession soon as their carcasses are out of deep water).

Thus the black woman is left to the limits of her own devices and unrelenting feelings of rejection, so that even when she is happily married, she is prone to see a black man's choice of a white woman as a personal rejection of her, the black woman; and it hurts all the more when the black man is a high profile black person or a "catch." Black psychiatrists William Grier and Price Cobbs once looked back over their many years of clinical work with black women and came to the daunting conclusion that: "one aspect of the black woman's life which attracts little attention from outsiders has to do with her hair. From the time of her birth, the little girl must submit to efforts aimed at changing the appearance of her hair. When she is a babe in arms her hair is brushed and stroked, but in short order the gentle brushing gives way to more vigorous brushing and ultimately combing. Her hair is kinky and combing is painful, but her mother must hold her and force her to submit to it. "

Troubled by these findings the black psychiatrists went on in *Black Rage* to give the tragic plight of the black woman a prominent place in their bestselling late Sixties book. The psychiatrists saw the black woman's poignant struggle with feminine narcissism and beauty as something akin to the epidemic condition emerging today that I am calling "Sexual Anorexia." "It may be," the black male psychiatrists wrote, "that after a brief struggle a black woman feels that femininity as it is defined in these times is something she cannot achieve. Rather than having her heart broken every day, she relinquishes the struggle and diverts her interests elsewhere. She has derived none of the intensely personal satisfaction she might have received as an honored and desirable sexual object."

As a possible fallout to the white woman's physiognomy as the standard of beauty for the black woman, from her head to her toe, Dr. Donda West, the black 58 year old Chicago State University English professor and mother of rap superstar Kanye West, died of complications of cosmetic surgery involving her deep and multiple somatic (or bodily) concerns. In response to Dr. West's untimely death, a black female California state legislator, Wilmer Carter, quickly introduced legislation ("the Donda West Law") which would require a medical clearance from a licensed physician before receiving cosmetic surgery, as reported by *Jet* magazine. It will very likely follow that a screening from a licensed psychologist or psychiatrist will be added to the clearance by a physician.

In another development believed partially related to problems of obesity and mental stress, a tripling of strokes in recent years has been found among middle-aged women in the United States, from 1999 to 2004, in a sample of women on medication to control blood pressure and cholesterol, according to AP reports summarized in *Jet*. As a matter of fact, the researchers found "that an increase in size of a woman's waistline corresponds with increase in strokes." However, it is also likely that the sample of women were suffering related anxieties about their obesity and their bodies (and some may also have been enduring spasms of sexual and political anorexia) as part of the cause and/or effect of the hike in strokes. This possibility is augmented by a recent study (reported in the *Los Angeles Times*) by professors at Harvard Medical School and the University of California at San Diego documenting "social contagion" in women's mindsets in the fact that the spread of obesity can be traced through a social network, something previously associated only with infectious physical diseases. Researchers found the influence of friends on weight

61

gain as powerful as the effects of genetics uncovered in other studies, and more than four times as powerful as the effect of siblings and spouses. Neighbors who weren't friends had no influence on one another, presumably indicating that the effect of social contagion from a social network may well trump lifestyle (including family eating habits) and genetics!

Yet while many black women refuse to give up the right to attract a viable black mate, they are compelled to come to grips with the fact that black males and females are held together by a bio-historical imperative: that the black man and woman exist primarily in the same pond; so that there may be an occasional scouring in the ocean for a different kind of fish but, in a political sense at least, the future of the black race demands that the future of the black woman will be with the black man just as surely as the future of the black man must be with the black woman.

It is no wonder, then that many black women find dating and mating more taxing than routine challenges such as job selection, house hunting, promotions, shopping, and church denomination. The serious sister operates on a systematic strategy: she records her needs, her expectations and a time-frame in which to achieve them. She knows joining her life and her body with someone will probably be the most serious mission she will ever undertake in her life.

Sociologist Robert Staples once outlined "The Role and Importance of Beauty in the Black Community" in *Black Male/Female Relationships,* a journal The Black Think Tank published from 1979 to 1982. Dr. Staples based his analysis on the findings of a *Jet* magazine survey of black women living in Chicago, on what black women see or look for in their choice of a man. According to Dr. Staples, black women demonstrated a strong preference for a physically attractive man and ranked the ten things they notice about men in this order: (1) Dress/grooming (2) personality (3) eyes (4) mouth/smile (5) money (6) physique (7) thoughtfulness/walk (8) intelligence (9) chest and (10) buttocks.

Lordy, Lordy. What manner of man will a woman get if she places things like how he dresses number one; his eyes, mouth, money and his physique above his thoughtfulness and intelligence (which trumped only his chest and his buttocks? Indeed, how many preferences that aren't physical do you see on the list? As a matter of fact, how much do we differ from black males in this skin color thing – except that we prefer the darker male and they the lighter woman? Remember in high school when a lot of girls said they didn't trust light skinned men? They associated dependability, the ability to settle down and good looking men with dark skinned men; they felt that dark skinned men were more settled, dependable and, oh yes, better looking.

We condemn black men for rating a woman by her physical features, but how much do we differ when we as black women focus on physical traits and fail to look at character? When the first black sorority was initiated some decades ago at Howard University (then referred to as "the capstone of Negro Education"), the qualities of skin color and hair were major prerequisites for entrance into the upper realm and status of Howard sisterhood -- much like a carry-over from the period of African American bondage, when the level and type of black employment was predicated on the master's sperm, skin color, and hair texture. The "big house" servants, the pale skins and the children of the plantation master were often the master's children (a fact frequently known but tolerated by the mistress looking the other way and seeking emotional refuge from her shame through the psychological mechanism of denial). Exploiting this legacy, the Alpha Kappa Alpha sorority had the pick of the litter, the "light, bright, damn near white." The second tier of the color ladder historically was claimed by the Delta Sigma Theta sorority, leaving the Zeta Phi Betas to recruit from the prototypes of Wallace Thurman's fictional characters in *The Blacker The Berry* ("the sweeter the juice"), before the coeds got the news that the blacker the college the sweeter the knowledge," based on lessons taught by such great black professors as: Carter G. Woodson, author of *The Miseducation of the Negro*; E. Franklin Frazier, in *Black Bourgeoisie*, and Nathan Hare, in *The Black Anglo Saxons*.

Today, after going through the black consciousness movement and postmodernism, a recently fashionable route for some young black women leads now increasingly to the cosmetic lip injections that Hollywood appears to regard as sexy in the white female but Aunt Jemima in the black female. The melanin-enriched black sisters with naturally pouty lips and full-size mouths are still considered repulsive or facially disfigured, despite all the praise afforded white counterparts such as "Pretty Woman's" white star Julia Roberts and America's ambassadorial sweetheart, Angelina Jolie. Meanwhile, now that these white women -- some with cosmetically assisted lips and butt injections --have become international red-carpet-stars, black women born with pouting lips and years of suffering the taunts and rejections of their physical features in an anti-black world are joining the frantic new rush for collagen injected fat lips. No wonder this is so, when we consider that both white and black employers continue to prefer the more middle class, lighter, whiter, personality in the office. They prefer to see the darker exiles from the underclass in debasing situation comedies, films, and television roles that lack high status, power, authority and prestige.

Happily the color complex is slowly changing. Serious sisters refuse to mimic the Hollywood standard of beauty and skin color. For their part, the time has come to recognize character, talent, intellect, integrity and spirituality. A black female president of a high-flying black women's organization makes it known that when she gets a hint of the old caste system creeping into her group, she puts the screws on it or promises to tender her resignation.

Yet antebellum slave styled practices continue to be visited upon the hair of black women. In Ayana D. Byrd and Lori L. Tharp's hilarious but sensitive, *Hair Story: Untangling the roots of Black Hair in America*, a woman spoke for millions of past and, lets hope, present and future sisters, when she lamented, "For years, I pushed, pounded, fried, dyed, re-fried, laid down, crocheted, braided, extended, Luster-curled, Jheri-curled, hot-combed, curling-ironed, and hair-rollered, trying to make sense to the rest of the world. " Why try to make sense to anybody but yourself. If you're satisfied with your tresses, your mane, extensions, ambience, and inborn splendor, you may require less high blood pressure medication. Add to that the disgracing fact that black women are caught up with the esthetics but not the economics of black hair, which remains an unfortunate fact and appears in turn to fuel the political anorexia preventing black economic control of the black hair industry. Recently an investigative documentary was produced and released about Korean control and distribution of black hair products. Most black people were already familiar with the thriving Asian controlled acrylic finger nail and pedicure business. Though the owners, managers and employees are Asian, seldom do you run into Asian customers in the nail shops. Why the Asian report shocked and angered black folk is a mystery and a state of denial. The black hair care industry (BHCI) has known and talked about this phenomenon for years --- dating back to the days of Dixie Peach hair pomade.

Why are so many blacks surprised that Koreans are controlling products only used by black folk? James Clingman, author, journalist and black economist, has railed for years in major black newspapers about the non-black-ownership of businesses populated mostly by black folk but owned by somebody else. Clingman sees the main point of the report revolving around another nationality's control over the economy of black dollars: "I do mean control, the overwhelming majority of the distribution and sale of Black hair care products which includes shampoos, conditioners, oils and creams, and those fashionable hairpieces our sisters love to wear." Clingman is even more incensed that we look on and even collaborate in the face of the demise of black control of an industry that continues to brag about Madame C. J. Walker, Annie Turnbo-Malone, Anthony Overton, S.B. Fuller and other black hair care pioneers, without a peep from black women's mouths." Clingman labels this black faux pas "The Black Hair Care Tragicomedy." We could get back control of our own cosmetics and come out of our political anorexia looking pretty, so to speak.

As things now stand, the heavy emotional toll of this negativity of color and hair crisis isn't visited upon white women with the intensity of the volley of degradation and rejection rained down on embattled black women. In the 2006 October issue of *First* magazine, a piece was devoted to how going blond brings instant success to many white female stars. Pictures showed Regis Filbert's co-host Kelly Ripa as a brunette in her soap opera role on "All My Children." Almost as soon as Kelly dyed her locks blond, she "clinched her current position as morning-show sidekick to Regis." Another before-and-after shot featured Meredith Viera when her hair was brown. The article told how when she went blond, "she caught the eye of producers and snagged her high profile job anchoring The Today Show on NBC." When a black woman goes blond (L'il Kim), she is immediately identified as a prostitute, a woman of the night, or at least a loose woman. Even though this perception of the blond black woman accrues from the fact that it is women of entertainment and the night that are most likely to wear blond wigs, black women who wear blond in the daytime are considered low life.

The magazine went on to list the perks of nonblack women going blond: "You'll be perceived as friendly before you even open your mouth." City University in London researchers found that the woman with blond hair is more extroverted. But in case you're wondering if you as a black woman should go blond, the writers warn that you must first have light eyes and thick hair --- no mention of fake light blue contact lenses. "Blond hair and light-colored eyes are both recessive (and therefore rare) genes, so they often go hand in hand. This has just exacerbated the political anorexia of black women and eliminated sisters from top TV slots.

Forgetting moments of scorn encountered in early life which can be cast aside quite easily by some women, but others carry these emotional scars to the grave. When black women see a dark-hued woman in a prominent position or enjoying national popularity, they hit the telephone lines and reminisce on how some things have gradually changed. When Whoopi Goldberg was at the apex of her popularity, black women whispered that she and others who resembled her -- even if publicly popular, wealthy and prominent -- would never be cast as Cinderella in the typical high school play.

The tragedy is that black teachers were many times the casting directors who did this in years past, who didn't want black children playing Cinderella roles. Dark-hued talents would count their blessings to play the wicked stepmother. A coffee-colored (without cream) public school teacher in Tulsa, Oklahoma used to curse her fate every morning when she glanced upon her reflection in the mirror. Teenaged students gathered in the bathroom would often look in the mirror and declare that the color-struck black teacher surely never looked at herself in the mirror and asked "mirror, mirror on the wall, who's the fairest of them all?" She must have known instinctively the mirror's answer would never court her favor. Even if the mirror wouldn't have been antagonistic to her over-abundant supply of melanin, she was caught up in her own programmed inferiority complex. It seems her low self esteem had settled in during the early days of her childhood, so that her angry confrontations with the mirror was but a retrospect of her youth translated into the self-hatred she transferred to the children who looked like her or reminded her of herself. Ironically she married a pharmacist who could easily pass for white. In her mind she had somehow escaped her color fixation. To paraphrase psychiatrist Frantz Fanon, in his classic on the psychology of oppression, *Black Skin, White Mask*: she appeared to believe that if she could be loved by the white man who is loved by the white woman, then she is white like the white woman, she is a full human being.

Unfortunately, in her role as the English teacher in an all-black school, she was also choreographer and director of school plays in which she featured only light skinned girls; their darker skinned peers were relegated to bit parts as housemaids, thieves, criminals, mobsters, supplicants and other roles of degradation. Hollywood could have used her, a dark-complected teacher, as casting director for the racist stereotypes they continue to perpetuate. The roles of Goldilocks (in *The Three Bears*) , Gretel (in *Hansen and Gretel*), Snow White and Little Red Riding Hood were reserved for children with skin tones like light-complexioned Halle Berry, Mariah Carey, Vanessa Williams, Niccole Riche and Beyonce Knowles.

I am certain the black school teacher never imagined the day would ever come when the world famous black African model, Alex Wek, would star in prestigious national and international white fashion rags and magazines, with major European and American designers literally at her feet. She has had a foot on every major runway in the world, sporting a bald, bold ego and strutting her stuff darkly. Still, sisters who are yet to arrive into the new millennium will huddle and giggle and whisper about her African visage and wonder out loud how in the world did it happen that a deep-black fleshed diva could ascend to commandeering the white fashion scene.

Such "Black Anglo Saxon" sisters stand appalled and perplexed when white femme fatales in Hollywood co-opt black women's hair styles. After Bo Derek copied and expropriated "cornrows," she was almost immediately touted as the most gorgeous "10" since Greta Garbo. While many black women have enjoyed and even profited from black hair styles, all has not been cotton candy sweet for black women. Major airlines went berserk when black flight attendants first came to work in their "dos." The airlines rationalized their sudden disgust on grounds that black hair styles would terrify white passengers, though several black afro-wearing flight attendants I know snagged a husband for themselves, not to mention trysts with somebody else's husband in their "do's."

Infuriated by this curious animosity many years ago, Dr. Regina Turner, a Bowling Green State University professor contacted the Black Think Tank, which was publishing the journal *Black Male/Female Relationships*, and sent us her article on "The Sexual Ordeal of the 'Ugly' Black Woman," which we immediately published in an issue whose cover featured an inquiry into "Why Black Men and Women Kill Each Other."

Although Prof. Turner was not a dark woman herself -- but perhaps too dark to be a backup singer for today's hip hop rappers -- she had told us of the many unpleasant confrontations and experiences she had suffered over her physical appearance from other children when she was a child. Truth hurts, but if you're an honest black woman you can also testify to many downbeat expressions aimed at children considered "unappealing."

69

"Lawd, you sho' is one ugly child." "You ain't nothing to look at, but…" "It' a good thing you smart." Or "Why couldn't you have looked like your brother?" Or "You look just like you ol' ugly daddy." Later, as an adult, Prof Turner was particularly taken aback when five educated brothers on separate occasions told her to her face without stuttering or stammering that she was physically hideous and unattractive. Makes you wonder who raised them.

After listening with the sensitivity and sophistication of a scholar to the black men in her sample, Prof Turner came up with what she called the "Ugly-Beautiful Continuum," in which she painstakingly composed a poignant list of what she called "sure indicators" of how some brothers pathetically measure sisters. It was a ponderous list: no curves. too skinny (well Diana Ross would have been eliminated in her heyday), big feet, flat feet (the late first lady Jackie Kennedy) overweight, knocked-knees, big eyes, big lips that get bigger when you get mad (but look how they love Angelina Jolie and Julia Roberts, with their unusually big lips, they stole husbands and became America's sweethearts), imperfect teeth, gaps (how do you eliminate the first black female Secretary of State, Lady Condoleeza) skin blemishes (hasn't everybody heard of hydroquinone?) broad shoulders (well Serena Williams has certainly made a lot of broad bank deposits). These brothers also included skinny legs, too tall, too short and, again, too dark (regardless of the temporary uplift in the late 1960s from the short-lived black consciousness movement.

One afternoon, I also witnessed a color complex scene that still gives me chills. It happened at a friend's family gathering of in-laws that took place in Oklahoma City, Oklahoma. On the day of the picnic the backyard was filled with laughter all day long, barbecuing and merrymaking, and everybody enjoying several generations of parents, cousins, step kin and church folk. Skin hues ranged from almost white to almost black. At one point I got up to look for the bathroom. The hostess pointed me in the right direction, back into the house and through the living room to the bathroom and down the hallway veering right. In the hallway a picture stretching almost half the length of the wall caught my eye. It gave me this feeling of déjà vu as by chance I had seen a copy of the photograph years before. It was a portrait of a tall handsome man (eerily resembling The Portrait of Dorian Gray), standing posed next to a dark and hefty black woman seated in an armchair, except that this time the tall man's hand rested on a shoulder that could have belonged to a black woman but the woman had now been cut out of the picture.

The hostess was also a heavyset dark woman. She was the granddaughter of the man in the picture frame and the blue-black woman seated in the photograph but her loving grandmother on whose shoulder the tall light and handsome grandfather's hand was resting, had now been removed. Somewhat bewildered, I stood looking long and furtively at the portrait in an effort to figure out what was missing. When the hostess caught me staring at the portrait, she poured on a cornucopia of excuses: "You know my grandfather was part white and part Indian," she proudly explained, "the others in the family don't want to admit he's half white and one-fourth black and one-fourth Indian, but I put his picture up for everybody to see. I'm not ashamed of him," she bragged.

When I realized she had cut her dark grandmother out of the picture – despite the fact that she herself was a replica of her grandmother – it was heartbreaking to me. For her to look at her grandmother 24/7 every day was apparently a bleak and insufferable reminder of her negative image of herself. I was not surprised to learn that she had long been troubled with sexual anorexia. She complained that in college there had often been many days when she couldn't get a date, until "Black History Month." Black males in her life had appeared to deepen her negative self image. In the absence of power over everything the white man does, some black males hooked up with light skinned black women until time and circumstances changed to permit them to date the "real" light-skinned woman, the white female, the lightest of the light.

A pitch dark sister told me one night in Las Vegas of her college days with an equally dark-skinned brother who began to ask her out to dances and to fraternity events and after-hour smooching sessions. She swore she had met the love of her life---the starting quarterback for the football team. I mean he was hot. Everybody knew him or lined up to meet him and the girls all drooled. But then the story ended. When he was on the way up and stuck in the sandlot league he dated dark girls, the darker the berry the sweeter the juice. Then came the touchdowns and the headlines and his headlong dash for white coeds.

First he dated the sister who thought she had met her future husband until he cast her aside and turned to fixate on light-skinned black women and eventually the white women who wanted his big-time jock perks and fame. Then he graduated from college and married a woman who already had several children by two different fathers. Almost as soon as he got drafted to the NFL, he was injured and cut from his team. When the team let him go she let him go, and he soon slipped into chronic alcoholism. At a college homecoming game that attracted the most successful alumni, he stumbled upon the now much acclaimed pitch black sister he had dumped for the white woman. Her past relationships with him and others from her college had turned her into a sexual anorexic. The men ran after her but she had given up the ghost of love and no longer had the heart for a monogamous relationship.

The color complex syndrome, if allowed, can produce contention between female friends to the point of complete alienation. Two black women I know were close friends with much in common but they were vastly different colors. One was a very short-haired well-rounded woman and the other was an extraordinarily light skinned long-haired shapely woman. Every time you saw one you saw the other. They had been friends since early childhood. Whispers were rampant among sisters and brothers in the community. Gossip had it that the dark-skinned woman always described as unattractive went around with this light skinned sister because she was thought to be attractive and, according to the tongue-wagging, the darker woman hung with her friend, hoping to be noticed and introduced to the men who flocked at the feet of the "beautiful one."

Throughout a white dominated society --- in schools, churches, employment, social activities – sociologists have long noted that the light skinned woman with straight locks is accorded preferential treatment. This has also been observed in politics. Think about it. Several people are running for office with similar platforms, each of them having no criminal records, no religious records and no public extra-marital sexual liaisons. The race will often be called in favor of the charismatic "looker," whether male or female; the most attractive candidate will often be appointed or elected.

Even the fashion industry caters to white society's definition of beauty: pants and jeans are not designed for the female buttocks of African lineage. Many black women have to purchase pants a couple of sizes larger to fit their hips, plus "pin" the waist. This may change now that white women are getting injections in their butts; and if this continues black women won't have to worry because then the seat of women's pants will be made larger.

Sisters often complain how prospective white male employers think black women gorgeous if thin, not too dark, have straight or straightened hair, "articulate" but should be seen more than heard. At a black male business seminar in a large Southern city, a panel of brothers addressing this physical issue mentioned some harsh realities that hadn't been taught in their college business classes. They testified that they were often hired and promoted on the basis of their physical features and the appearance of their wives. It seems that when the company parties and weekend cocktail events are held, the men who come with wives or girl friends regarded as unattractive by Western standards tend to be ignored.

Some single men exploiting this situation adopt a strategy of what a Howard University counselor Audrey Chapman calls the "a la carte approach" to dating – and many women in desperation are starting to adopt this "radical new way of relating to the men in your life." The *a la carte* approach to dating is like *a la carte* in a restaurant; you pick what you want, this from this entre, that from this side dish, something else for the appetizer.   In *a la carte* dating, you pick one man for a public escort, another for sex (often somebody you'd be ashamed to introduce to your girlfriends), another man for companionship, and another for his credit cards and perks. Of course you may pay a little more, but think it's worth it for a flicker of happiness.

These women are attempting to cope with the male smorgasbord. One black male I know enjoys a copious stable of female friends; he selects his dates as some would choose their attire, based on the particular function. Is the party for international sales people, corporate directors and politicians funded by the corporation, or wives of major CEOs? As soon as he learns the nature of the gathering he peeps in his little black book to find the right black female fit. He has the women divided into categories. One type may be invited for physical fitness activities such as golf or tennis. Another type might seem more appropriate for the company's annual employee or stock holder's cruise. In any case, the woman picked out for the company cruise is carefully scrutinized. When the man is doing the picking for his company date, she's often picked on how she looks in a thong or a bikini. He knows that all male eyes will trail her but this gives him a moment to play the field and one-up other men.

Try spending several days at sea with someone if you are curious about their pedigree or the quality of their behavior. You'll learn more from that experience than tea leaf readers. Most people can't keep up a pretense for the duration of the cruise, slipping into Ebonics as the liquor loosens the tongue; four letter words have been known to be directed to the CEO and other company officials. You have never seen somebody act or turn into a fool until you have spent several days at sea with these people. The liquor flows 24/7, the "get down tonight" music blares all night. Women as well as men often wear just enough to keep from getting arrested. All the staterooms (bedrooms) begin to look alike; relatives as well as strangers often end up wrapped under the same covers and may wake up in bed with the company CEO or, God forbid, his wife. The next morning there are those too hung over to get over the hang- over. This is why the black male choosing a black woman to go on a cruise all but goes to the convent for his choice of a sister.

Back in 1966 when black folk were asserting their African heritage and Afro-American dignity, Howard University was graced with its first football queen who would dare to sport an Afro hairdo. You'd think such an historical moment as that would unleash pride and dancing in the streets. Not quite. Howard administrators recoiled in horror, writhing in collective angina pangs reminiscent of someone forced to go from caviar to pig's feet. This was an institution priding itself on being called "the Black Harvard." These University overseers rushed in to bolster their disdain for "natural black hair," an acknowledgement of being black and proud. To have the Howard University queen sporting an afro was a depravity and a disaster in the minds of the administrators. They were afraid it would get to the media, to the public, to their benefactors and their bread-and-butter financiers, including white Southern federal officials in the District of Columbia

The Howard administrators and the "Academic Uncle Toms" hurried and scurried to stop what students and faculty saw as progress. To the administration, choosing an African American queen was like creating a plantation insurrection. They were exhibiting what Richard Wright described in *Native Son* as a choice "between amputation and Gangrene." "Chocolate City" won. Only history will tell if that historic struggle on the elite campus has continued, not to the exclusion of our light skin sister, but to incorporate high melanin endowed sisters into the exhibition gallery at Howard and other "historically black" college campus caravans of queens.

This brings us to the Comb Test about which there are still conflicting reports. Opinions and research are not the same. Scholars prefer research to validate their statements. Down home black folk trust personal experiences and observations to validate their conclusions. Some historians say the Comb Test literally existed; others claim it to have been invisible to the eye but ever present in the psyche. It's like not seeing the wind but feeling its bone-chilling presence.

Bards and troubadours of the time often told the story of "silk stocking churches" requiring the comb test. If the comb could pass through your hair without stalling in your "kitchen" (not the one with the cooking stove - it's the one where the hair meets the neck) you were IN. The Brown Paper Bag Test was also integrated with the Comb Test, meaning your complexion had to be at least one shade lighter than a paper bag, if you wished to partake of the Holy Eucharist with these well positioned high heeled parishioners.

With all this stress and mental indigestion behind color and hair, no wonder the black woman has remained in the aesthetic second class. In November 2006 issue of *Allure* magazine, Winnie Holzman explores the widespread "Dreaming of Good Hair." A white woman had spent years fighting frizzy locks while hoping for straight hair. She was quoted as saying "This isn't my hair. I can no longer be silent." And she did not stand still. She went to a salon and had her hair chemically relaxed to the tune of $400 dollars. Now she says, "This is my hair on drugs." Her real natural hair was curly. She referred to it as Frizzy curly, fuzzy curly, Jewish curly.

She went to a Japanese hair-relaxing salon to have her hair "transformed from curly and frizzy to silky and amazing." She finally had something she'd "wanted since birth." She still wondered why Japanese people who are assumed to have straight hair, would know how to rid folks heads of kink, frizz and unwanted curls. She was told that some Japanese have "difficult" hair. But this is what she said: "if you're Japanese with coarse hair, you've got a problem. It's called mortification." Ms. Holzman worked for television, where she also "noticed that on TV there is only "good" hair." "Bad hair isn't just rare on television – it's the only real taboo left." She never mentioned all of the fake extensions almost every white female anchor is sitting there flaunting, while flinging the extensions constantly or pushing them back with one hand constantly pretending to keep out of their faces while pulling their too-short skirt down repetitively with their other hand.

Could this "bad hair" taboo be the explanation for the rarity of black female news anchors? Does this explain why the high paid chatter boxes on talk shows are seldom black? If black women feel helpless and hopeless to stop this genetic DNA racism, political and sexual anorexia will continue to increase to pandemic proportions.

Part II
POLITICAL ANOREXIA

Chapter 4

Male Carriers of the Virus of Sexual Anorexia

Beyond the fight for love and glory and the double whammy of racial and sexual oppression, the black woman is victimized by forces within her social order and herself. One undeniable dynamic that traumatizes and places her at risk is the quality of the character and relations of the men in her life – leaving aside for a moment the fact that they are operating in a situation of captivity, descendants of slaves who were forbidden to marry and whose women and children were split up and sold away from them and their wives and mothers at the master's whim.

The Many Ways Men Pimp Their Women

From the time Sampson fell prey to the love of Delilah and Cleopatra, the dark Egyptian beauty who captured the hearts of Julius Caesar and Mark Antony, down to the present day, men have struggled with their fear, their dread of women, lost their minds and gone to their deaths in vain attempts to cope with the endless war of the sexes. Yet they are capable of deep admiration and devotion to women; and maybe that is where it all begins, this paradox, this desire of the man to dominate and exploit the woman in the process of loving her.

To cut to the chase, we can say that men fall roughly into four main personality types in the power struggle between male and female (not limited to black males but gender-wide). According to our research at the

Black Think Tank and our observations in the Kupenda black love groups circa 1980, as well as in the clinical situation, these men may be recognized and categorized as follows:

1) **King Narcissus** (Don Juan, Super Fly, Pretty Boy Floyd),who can love only himself but collects women in his futile effort to prove that everybody loves him too, or that he is as lovable as he longs to be.

2) **Dr. Jekyll and Mr. Hyde** (a split personality), who can be one thing to a woman today but is quite another tomorrow, often consciously employing the street pimp's "kiss-kick" principle of brainwashing, where mean mistreatment is mingled with syrupy sweetness.

3) **Napoleon Bonaparte** (Bad, Bad Leroy Brown), the macho tyrant, domineering and super-sexist, whose main desire is to subordinate the women who are caught in his harem and to extend his empire.

4) **Nero the Fiddler** (Cool Breeze, Sweet Daddy, Iceberg Slim) who fiddles while his mate labors for her pay, either disdaining economic enterprise altogether or bouncing from one university to another, never graduating, or from one petty activity to another, yet holding out the hope of someday making it big (in gross contrast to the man with true talent or ability who actually is trying to launch a career).

These four personality types have much in common including a view of women as mysterious and somehow capable of snaring and destroying men. This view of women as secretly dreadful beings is in part a product of a man's inability in childhood to fathom mother, which is where the "cupboard theory" advanced by psychoanalysts, comes in. Such men thus impute a godlike quality to women, but,

82

according to some women, nevertheless treat their women like the devil or something other than sugar and spice. Let us meet them one by one.

King Narcissus. Although not necessarily the most brutal, King Narcissus is perhaps the type that brings the greatest agony. Sistas complain that even single or unattached men (a rarity at any given moment, though some will tell you for a one night stand or even a little while longer that they are not married), are all too reluctant to make a genuine commitment to a woman. They delight in exploiting the shortage of eligible males in the marriageable age group, particularly in the middle classes. "They're having a field day up in here," a California barmaid once said to me.

Other Sistas complain for days about the ever exploding popularity of young professional lounges and the simultaneous emergence of a kind of "bourgeois pimp" exploding on the scene. The "bourgie pimp" is inclined to "lurk in body bars and similar places, mind you never buying drinks but hustling them from you or any lonely woman who might chance to come there – and you know they will -- looking for a hope-to-die kind of love. These women arrive there in their loneliness, love-starved and demoralized condition ready to pounce on a man, but "it's the women who seem to wind up hurt."

Usually King Narcissus is already tied to some woman before he gets to the bar, but it's when he isn't we're talking about, because that's when he comes in "scoping," poised and ready to clamp his chops on the lonely and receptive women who are all too ready to be flowered with sympathy and to swallow their married lover man's story ("Aw, he can be a tear-jerker," Sistas will tell you," explaining why they invest such false and unrequited hopes in the King (who often refers to them as "My Queen") only to discover that your King has miraculously resolved his marital grievances with his so-called hateful wife and is working his way back home.

And you wonder why some Sistas are beginning to feel that casual or irresponsible sex ("sex without sentiment") is now almost synonymous with the masculine point of view, despite the fact that the double standard (once symbolized by the chastity belt) continues to leave men much less tolerant of infidelity on the part of their women than women are of their men. In the shadows of underground love there is even "wife-swapping" – but never husband swapping -- unless you mean in the cases when so many women jump up and marry one another's castoffs and "losers" -- but there is no phrase for husband swapping, though it seems there soon will be, judging by the way it is being practiced undercover in all the surreptitious ways that occasionally come to light.

Some men like King Narcissus are psychologically driven to seek reassurance of their masculinity through multiple female relationships, collecting women (and sometimes their assets) in a quest for symbolic masculinity. This acquisitive drive of the male may have deeper psychological roots beyond his social circumstances and may be tied to the bio-cultural bond of mother and infant, where the mother, a woman, is the first love object and chief caretaker for boys and girls, typically replaced by other women in nurseries, preschools and early school life. As previously indicated, psychoanalysts have labeled this the "cupboard theory," which holds that men in adulthood relationships will act out their secret desires and longings, their most primitive and infantile conflicts with their mothers, in their relationships with their women.

Needless to say, this kind of brotha is evil when he is with his woman but jealous when they are apart. They are best noted for their use of what pimps call "the love-hate" principle of relating to a woman, that is, mixing sporadic meanness with nocturnal sweet good loving. They exploit a woman's need to feel desired and desirable, using slick sweet talk and related sweetening ploys to dissolve her resistance or elicit her submission and compliance. He tells you "what you look good in, Girl; he plays with your kids, gets on good with your momma, talks about maybe getting married, while he is moving all the while to take over your life completely, before he quits his job or goes on the prowl for anything wearing a miniskirt and thongs."

Napoleon Bonaparte. This orientation of a brother grows directly out of his situation of oppression, but goes beyond the conventional misplacement of rage, according to psychoanalysts. Studies of the psychological fears of men and women show men to be fearful of castration and impotence while women exhibit anxiety over loss of love and the possibility of being left on the shelf. Unlike the female, who's anxiety tends to resolve around her need to be desired and desirable, the male's psychological component or challenge in the sexual encounter is to gain and hold an erection, that is to show up and rise to the occasion: if he's singing "you know my starter won't start this morning," you know he's got the blues. But, in the annals of psychoanalysis, a man's ability to attract a woman may pivot more on his "social potency," his social power, that is, his social position, his prestige, his wealth, than on his physical prowess. The black male, blocked from the avenues to social potency may be impelled to overcompensate in the sexual. Like the Napoleon Bonaparte lover man, he may see his "net worth" primarily in terms of his capacities in "the sack" which he mistakenly believes to be equivalent only to how well he is "endowed," in terms of his physical assets, compounded by the number of women he can snare, so that his masculinity is measured by his ability to hunt down and subdue as many women as possible, augmented by his ability to exercise dominance and dominion over his prey. He wishes to achieve total control over his women – never closing the books on just one woman – seeking in every woman the control he could not exercise in his infancy, to be the little dictator he could not be with his mother.

Achieving control over one woman is but the kicker to a compulsion to extend his domain in order to exercise his infantile wish. For a woman to evade his dominance is a threat to his masculinity, if not "castrating" to him, so he must keep her in a "prone position." She may even be admonished not to disagree with him or otherwise violate his manly prerogatives, especially in public places or anywhere else in the company of others. "You'd think that if a woman makes more money than a man that would mean the whole family could live a little better," a Sista confided to me. "But instead there's a constant hassle because her paycheck is bigger than his and he feels threatened, but all the time he's out there somewhere using the money and even taking part of it to buy some other woman drinks and talking about "set 'm up" for anybody he can.

Nero the Fiddler. Nero may be a fiddling emperor, but he is no less manipulative, because he is also consumed by the passion to resurrect with the object of his affection, the extension of his mother, the same symbiotic if not parasitic bond of his lost but unresolved early mother-child relationship. He is encouraged by the fact that the old tradition of the "kept woman" is vanishing in the throes of contemporary feminine advancement and fading male financial incapacity (giving rise to an increasing social acceptance of the "house husband" or the "kept man").

Nero often moves in with a woman by calculated degrees; first staying overnight to "test the water" and "make sure the coast is clear." Say one night he brings along some extra clothing and toiletries, a toothbrush and the like, so on Friday he can come straight there from work, pleading haste, and dress for some special date or dinner dance. It doesn't take long before it's "hey, Mama, I see you already pay a lot of rent here…I might just move in wit' you and help you out wit' loose ends and stuff." After a few flattering routines of praise for her cooking – in preference to "eating out" on the money he doesn't have -- the dinner outings vanish. Instead he fiddles (e.g. watches television or plays with her computer and the internet while she cleans the house, cooks the food, serves the table, wash the dishes, empties the trash, mops the floor, watches the kids, fusses with him, keeps herself up, tries to look attractive and satisfies his needs)."

Fact is "Bro" acquires a bundle of services, stone free, from his "queen," the woman of the house – servant, hostess, dietician, social secretary, nurse, nursemaid, typist, editor, governess, all the things he's used to getting with his mother, in whose house these days he often has been staying before he got to you. What used to be called a "help meet" (helping him to meet the bills, or serving as doctor's wife, mayor's wife, pastor's wife, all of this *gratis*) today is referred to as "logistical support" in pimp lingo by the allegedly sophisticated computer literate postmodern man who would be "kept" by the woman while preparing to cross the "digital divide." Lest we forget, "logistical support" includes "in-house services" as well as outside obligations that might even earn a sista a P.H.T. degree , Putting Hubby Through school.

Where a man used to put an engagement ring on a woman's finger to get close to her and her goodies (that is, access the privileges supposedly reserved for the sanctuary of marriage), now marriage has lost some of its status and sanctity (especially in the mind of the young black male, relatively speaking, studies show). In today's culture of liberation, many men continue to "tie the knot" and to urge a wedding ring upon a wife to symbolize for any would-be suitors the fact that she is already "tied up" or "taken," at least tentatively, while he keeps his fingers free to play and fiddle.

Men Who Fear Love

Women have felt for some time that there are men who suffer an acute fear of loving, a revulsion to a commitment to just one woman and a serious emotional involvement. When naïve or unsuspecting women meet these men they usually have no idea what they have just tangled with: the kind of man a shrink might call amoraphobic (fear and or hatred of love).

The men we are calling amoraphobic are emotionally crippled by neurotic fears of getting too close to a woman. Fearing to make the romantic struggle with any one woman, they seek safety in a multiplicity of women and find it hard to keep their commitment to any one woman; they skip from woman to woman and sometimes man to man.

Because there is a surplus of black women, many black men feel they don't have to put out as much and will even remind the woman grappling with the man shortage – "don't forget there's a black male shortage up in here" – and will tell her pointblank: "take care of your homework, Baby, if you don't, somebody will" (by homework they customarily mean anything they want her to do, in and outside of the home). Many feel they are messiahs placed on earth and sent here to "service an abundance of women" and to help women through the black male shortage. Understandably this didn't take long to create a new black male narcissism. It used to be that you could walk through the black community and see a lot of pretty women and a lot of working men; now you go through the black community and see a lot of working women and a lot of pretty men.

Bolstered by black female horror over the hovering image of the much bemoaned and talked about "black male shortage," the successful black man – or even a brother with a regular job and side benefits -- will often gain an elevated sense of importance, becoming amoraphobic.

The amoraphobic male is likely to be caught up in a need to avoid what he abhors and fears even though his appetite for sex may remain enormous. He is representative of a category of men we often saw in the Black Think Tank's "Kupenda" ("black love") groups; in time we came to call them Apollomaniacs.

Apollomaniacs are a variety of amoraphobics obsessed with a narcissistic scramble for a horde of women, but their obsessive zeal is but a quest for sexual intimacy as psychological compensation for deeper feelings of emotional estrangement. Despite their state of chronic insatiability, they appear incessantly to be looking for their mothers in every woman. Thus they are hooked on the horns of an emotional dilemma, a seesaw of adjustment and maladjustment, caught in a helter-skelter sex-driven love life, tangled in the gap between desire for sexual variety and the need for psychological and social stability.

Yet feeling rejected and unadjusted, despite the physical rewards of their boundless search for pleasure and masculine validation, they must live with an uneasy suspicion that they do not measure up as a man or a lover to the task of making and sustaining a serious relationship.

But let us return to the amoraphobics proper. Like the pimps he wishes to emulate, the amoraphobic male endeavors to hide behind an unfathomable fear of intimacy that interferes with his pimp-based façade of sexual efficacy and proficiency. He rejects the women he fears will reject him. While the pimp prefers to turn the tables on the woman (reversing those roles he believes diminish him), the amoraphobic is turning his back on the women he fears may violate him emotionally if he gets too close or takes any chance on love. Thus many of the amoraphobics -- who will focus on one woman on a periodic basis -- will wear out their welcome with a woman and even punctuate their sojourn with stormy fits of jealousy and interpersonal fury.

Much in the manner of the man on death row who killed nine women and then no more after finally and actually killing his mother, the amoraphobic's problems may have started in childhood. Too many black men, when they were children, had to suffer the loss of their fathers through incarceration divorce or desertion. Others had fathers who were present in the home yet psychologically unavailable to them; so that sometimes, even when the amoraphobic is a model of manly deportment and disciplinary devotion, he is likely to have unresolved conflicts with his mother (the opposite-sex parent) who was left alone to be both mother and father to him, although camouflaged in the role of a single parent.

Within these fatherless circumstances there is likely to emerge ambivalence and uncertainty in the boy, aggravated in turn by a resentment born of resistance to the mother's double-duty functions and responsibilities as sole disciplinarian and authority figure. These unresolved conflicts with the mother will follow him into his adult encounters with the women he will love and marry -- extensions of his mother. His approach to the woman he would love is complicated by what psychoanalyst Helen Bloch, in *The War Between the Sexes*, called "the cupboard syndrome." Women in the mind of the amoraphobic symbolize his mother, or a kind of cupboard from which to gain nurturance and goodies but at the same time remains the one who whacks his hand out of the cookie jar, leaving him with feelings of conflict, of victimization, of hostility and unrequited revenge.

It is in this way that a single mother, who is the singular disciplinarian, can become confused and equated in a boy's mind with the harshness that compounds his feelings of rejection by the psychologically unavailable or absent father. It is this circumstance that may inadvertently feed in him an inclination to over-identify with the mother, even while locked in feelings of the inappropriate and horrific nature of his attachment . In time the boy may surrender the struggle to love a woman altogether to a compulsion to imitate or usurp the woman's role in romantic relationships in a reversal of roles, much like the pimp who may rise to the apex of masculinity and sexual prowess in the ways of ultra-masculine female domination. In the observation of the black linguistic psychologist Dr. Ernie Smith, the boy on the road to becoming a pimp will long perhaps unconsciously to "turn the tables on the woman," saying in effect: "if I am in fear of women or the love of women or have given up on the hope of being truly loved by the women with whom I must fight out my unresolved conflicts with my mother, "I will turn the tables; I will be the pretty one; I will be kept like a woman, resting by day and dressing by night; in fact I will be kept by the woman." In a kind of psychological warfare ("the mind game"), the pimp mixes syrupy sweetness with mean mistreatment in the thought control they exercise over the women in their stable.

Not surprisingly pimps such as Iceberg Slim have confessed to a certain hatred of women, while feeling that their mothers had turned them into pimps by prematurely anointing them as precocious pseudo-sexual objects: "Ain't he cute. He's go'n be a heartbreaker . I'm go'n show him how to deal with these bitches and hos." For other men of the amoraphobic variety, perhaps the model group, the mother may unconsciously transmit a feminine way of coping which unfits a boy for the challenge of contending in the labor force and marketplace, or being an adaptive man, but also may lead to feminine behavior in his relationships with women: dependency, helplessness, passivity, even passive-aggressive ways of dealing with interpersonal conflicts, particularly with the opposite sex. This includes such strategies as pouting and the silent brooding that masks a woman's many untold hurts that often unconsciously break out in antagonistic and subtle ways. This masculine co-optation of the qualities of the feminine found in the very prototype of the pimp himself, relegates a man to the frame of mind that may feed a natural inclination if not an expectation of being caressed and pampered by a woman.

Within this state of affairs a woman loses a portion of her uniqueness, something special is taken away, along with her own importance to a man who keeps one eye on the door and another on some other woman, his head spinning with intoxicating visions of foxy queued up women. Fueled moreover by smiles and come-hither clothes of emancipated women he meets on crowded city streets (he mistakenly believes that the women who smile and flirt with him as he walks down the street would be available to him on demand if he could get to know them). Many men take this expectation so much for granted they operate on a sense of entitlement, so that they will angrily berate a Sista who refuses to speak to them in response to their idle flirtations in the streets; she has assaulted a part of his ego and his sense of his place in the hierarchy of a woman's needs and wants in the midst of a real or imagined black male dearth and the scanty quality of the "marriageable" black male supply. Which, translated into the logic of his heady fantasies means that just about every black woman is craving his company and would love to marry him, never hearing the women saying "he ain't all that." True, as *Ebony* magazine has perennially reported, "eligible bachelors" and marriageable black males ("those who are educated and well employed") are "few in number and, naturally, in the most demand." These men are likely to be the ones *Ebony* magazine had in mind when they wrote of "the spoiled ones."

Although fully masculine, even macho in every other respect, such men come to their relationships with women, miscued if not mismatched. At best, their relationships will be like two left shoes. Amoraphobics, however, are unaware of what is wrong, let alone what they themselves do wrong. It is the mate who, in their minds, is out of sync, producing chronic bitterness and outrage which only serve to compound already conflicted relationships. Amoraphobics may "hurt so bad" they "feel like a ballgame on a rainy day," as one blues singer put it. They approach women as a man wrapped in a wet blanket would approach an electric wire in a nuclear power plant. In their relationships with their women, they are forever in the hot seat. Sometimes men who play are trying to take on the persona of a street pimp as a way of fostering their unfulfilled ego deficits and manhood strivings.

Men Who Play

Why do black men play? Since there is a shortage of black men and white men are not lined up to be with black women, black men have the pick of the litter. Some black men actually seem to feel they're doing a favor to women who are out there lonely without a man, just looking for companionship. Such men don't know or understand how much they are contributing to the sexual anorexia of the black woman. Because she doesn't know that he's out there "servicing" all of these other women, she believes that she is the one he's chosen, thinking she's his one and only. He's having a good time now that he's moving on up in the socioeconomic world with an A.A. degree, a high profile job and dressing in designers tailored suits. He has abandoned the white socks of his childhood for long socks up to his knees, and shoes no longer begging to go to the shoe repair shop or the waste basket. – He now gets the kind of woman who would never have looked at him in his youth.

Let your eyes and your memories take you back to your high school queen and your fraternity sweethearts when women were not chosen for scholarship and intelligence. They were chosen on the basis of a European standard of beauty, how close they could get to Snow White or Cinderella. But alas, we return to reunions to find that we can't recognize these queens who have lost their thrones and everything that once caused them to be the chosen ones. Instead they have added pounds of uncomely body fat and let their hair and their appearance go bad, partly because they never had to worry or work at making themselves attractive, didn't have to learn and master and endure the straightening combs, the lipstick and the eyeliners, they thought their *au naturalle* would last forever, forgetting that beauty is fleeting if you don't work at it.

Once while I was chairing a meeting of young black males in Ohio, the black male shortage became a hot topic on the agenda. One man stood and said to the cheers of the others, "Man, just wait and get you an education and a job and you won't want the women who don't want you now." Some of the older brothers at the conference went on basking in rhetoric of "the black male shortage" and how they had these big-time jobs, ready and willing to take advantage of the abundant supply of black females. A freshman student in horn-rimmed glasses from a nearby college got up and complained that his older brethren seemed to have a

94

pick of the women while he couldn't get anybody. The women ignored him, but the brothas fell all over themselves advising him to "wait until you get your degree and get a job and a good looking suit and a new pair of shoes without the heels creeled over, and a brand new car, and women will be falling all over you."

A lot of this playing and the reason men play is because they were rejected in their youth. In *How to Find and Keep a BMW* (Black Man Working), we addressed what we called the "Superfly Syndrome" by contrast to the nerdy Booker T. Washington type. Females in the adolescent culture of the ghetto tend to be attracted to the most popular boy, often best dancer, the best rapper, somebody who can talk that talk and walk that walk, the embryonic polygamist. A woman is all too likely to shut her eyes to all the competition she will have, because she wants the boy the other girls want. She skips over the horn-rimmed "A student, the Booker T. type, with his pants too short or flooding, the toes of his shoes turned up and unpolished, knowing all the answers to the teacher's questions, always sitting up there in the very front row, far from all the back row social mischief and "making out."

The irony is that once the women are adults and have to face the bear and work and pay house notes and rent and buy clothes, they eventually reach the point when hipsters, the Superflies, the hip-hoppers and up-and-coming rappers no longer suit their lifestyle or fancy. With women who are highly successful, the more successful they become the harder it is to find the kind of man who is responsible enough to match and mediate her upward social mobility, so she comes to the realization, "I can have nothing all by myself." And they're not looking for man-sharing a piece of a man, they want a whole man they can call their own, a man who either has something or wants something (a man who is looking for social and economic potency).

95

Many of the women at a certain level may share a man, say the man of one of their friends, sometimes their best friend's man, sometimes knowingly but most of the time unknowingly. Sometimes the women in her circle will know she is dating one of their husbands, because they talk and there is no such thing as a secret among two desperate women unless one is dead, unless one person is dead.

A lot of men who play had a bad relationship with their mothers and are working out their unresolved conflicts with their mothers with their wives, women and playmates. Psychology conspires with history to tell us why some of these men do play. A lot of men of high repute have sauntered into our clinical offices after getting their lives and relationships tangled in their ineffectual meanderings in the ill-gotten harvests of players. It is a frequent occurrence for these men to get into longwinded confessions of the fury that has complicated their interpersonal relations and twisted their love lives due to their undying frustrations and regrets from the simple fact that growing up they didn't get along with their mothers.

Sistas think it's mostly the street pimps and corner boys that do all of the playing, so they forget about the preachers and high profile types they think can do more for them than the men who put them up in cheap hotels. High level men who play often send their woman ahead on business trips by first class plane so when they get there the suite and the sweetie will be waiting. Plus in case anybody sees them getting off the plane together they can't say they saw them traveling together. Quite a few preachers are known for this.

However, the poor man , the corner hustler who plays, is very often a brother who is looking for somebody to take care of him. The sister thinks the socially potent brother can introduce her to a style of life to which she is unaccustomed.. The upper middle class woman is looking for a man to take care of her, or at least to accommodate her own accumulations. She's more likely to go after the high profile men who play, a brother who knows that if he plays he must pay. Many times her grandmother has taught her never to go with a married man , or even a single man, "who doesn't have more to lose than you do." Then if the relationship falls apart, the player, being a man of means, will have to pay and often it will be paid in public, because her motto is: "If I go down, you're coming too."

The high profile woman is likely to be a shrewd sister who goes after a high profile man knowing that man is married because she is no amateur, she's experienced. Not that there aren't women who play, but women who play often have children and maternal obligations. They have to make sure their children are cared for when they're out on a rendezvous. Not infrequently the primary care giver, she has to tuck her children into bed and see that they get up and out to school mornings and can't stay out all night. Her relationships tend to be silhouetted in the shadows of daylight. She prefers not to be keeping her man out late and breaking up somebody's happy home and family in the midst of her indiscretions, so she endeavors to be careful when she goes out to play.

The down low brother not only plays, he double dips; and. because of the AIDS pandemic, is more dangerous to her health. This brother is often a high achiever, tenured professor, outstanding musician, artist, elected official, preacher, a high profile pillar of the community. While he does not necessarily desire a woman per se, he is highly familiar with a woman's desires. He is often steeped in chivalry, knows how to get up from his seat when she walks in, opens doors, remembers holidays and birthdays, sends roses, and knows what to buy and do to please the tastes of the woman who for the first time in her life is unknowingly competing with a another man. So many women are delighted to get the treatment, courtesy, graciousness, and basic good manners, if not the gallantry and courtliness they seldom receive these days from the straight men in their lives.

A lot of women don't want to admit this, but they know who the players are in the black community. The grape vine in black female circles runs around the clock. Many women have heard their girlfriends say they've been out with these men and yet they turn around and go out with these same men. After hearing all about another woman's man, always taking her to five-star hotels and restaurants, buying her expenses jewels and gifts, a woman accustomed to only eat-all-you-can dinner dates will often be overcome with envy and want these things for herself or to "get back at the bragging heifer," so she goes after the heralded man of her friend, unbeknownst to the friend. To escape from their frustrated and lonely, they will go for these men, if only for a passing moment. They wish for the excitement and the thrill of it all. These women also know that no one can talk that talk and walk that walk like the men who play.

One sister approached a player she'd been dating and told him she'd heard from her girlfriends he'd been running around with somebody else. Experienced like players are in knowing what to do when they're found out, the man replied: "you knew what I was when you took up with me." Because of experiences like these, a woman can all too easily fall into raging emotional rivers of sexual anorexia and its feelings of agony and victimization, never realizing how often she has brought it on herself, because she knew what this man was like when she met him.

Meanwhile, the sexual anorexia of the black woman rages on.

Chapter 5

Why Black Women Find It Hard to

Work with White Women

If it can be said that the black man is often a thorn in the black woman's side, and the white man is a wrench on her back and a load on her life and her race, it might readily appear to be convenient for the black woman to place her lot with the white woman. After all, the black woman and the white woman are rooted in gender and also came face to face for centuries in the intimate entanglements of nursemaid and housecleaning on the slave plantation in ways unavailable to the white master and his black male slaves. Yet it was the nature of the relationship of mistress and slave that quickly filled the black woman with a reservoir of resentment at the same time as the white woman on occasion felt secret pangs of envy for the black women taken as objects of her husband's lustful ewl desires when he exploited a black slave woman as an involuntary sex toy or concubine, sometimes on the pretense of breeding more slaves for the care and feeding of the mistress and her family.

Recorded history is relatively silent on the white woman's reactions to the sexual liaisons of black slave women and white slave masters, but it appears that white women generally looked the other way. Also, oral accounts from black grandmothers and great-grands who were slaves have passed on family secrets and revelations about these trysts that richly reveal the white man's vile and vicious attraction and grimy hunger for the black woman's pleasures. Indeed, there is testimony that these matters quite often became the source of argument between master and mistress and even a cause for punishment of the black slave woman or concubine by the white plantation mistress as well as pressures on the master from the mistress to sell the black concubine down the river, even if it meant snatching her away from her children (often sired by the master) and leaving them behind, not to mention taking her half-white telltale children and selling them away from her.

I have firsthand testimony from persons who have seen the tunnel leading from the bedroom of Thomas Jefferson (the great statesman and historically renowned contributor to miscegenation) to his Monticello mansion on a lordly Virginia mountain. Both folklore and history are replete with testimony to the fact that black women on many occasions had to watch their men savagely hanged allegedly for raping some white woman, which hurt all the more when it was known that the sexual allegations were not true, when a black man in actuality would be lynched for getting out of line or in victorious combat with a white man, even though it would often be based on false allegations of rape or a rape performed by another black man who had managed to evade the bloodthirsty lynch mob. Despite its entanglement in the intricacies of race and sex, the political relationship of the black woman and the white woman is if anything more complicated and more intimately entwined with the alienation of the black woman and the white woman, and this stretches back from the corridors of antebellum slavery down to the present day of closeted corporate office politics and sex in the city.

Nevertheless I was somewhat taken aback one day when two corporate white women walked up to me at a black women's conference and asked me why black women find it hard to work with white women. Black women have also asked me why white women find it hard to work with them. This does not surprise me based on my experiences working with black women, working with all white women, and working with them both when they are mixed.

I once worked for a company with six highly educated black women employed in low and mid-level positions subordinate to thirty-seven less educated white women, some in top management, but they would all gather in the coffee canteen section to gossip over the usual "who's zooming who" to get a promotion. One day one of the two white women cocked her head and fell to boasting of how she hadn't worked in ten years before she finally accepted an invitation to come there in one of the top managerial positions, "just to get out of the house and have extra spending change for tummy tucks, breast implants, and cosmetic makeovers." The black women were stunned that she would admit this in the presence of black female underlings stuck in their same entry level positions with hardly enough money for a cheap lipstick from the corner drug store. Now the white women had been hired into these top management positions with neither the skill nor the education required. The CEO, a white man, simply delegated the training of these women to three black women who, taken together, had shared twenty long years with the company and had been in the running for these same high positions long before the white women came on the scene, but kept being told they needed more experience.

If more experience was needed, why were they ordered to train the white women with no experience at all? Who wouldn't be enraged, with years of experience, to have to train someone with no experience to be their boss? If you can train the new hires for top positions and salaries, you deserve to be the boss. One of the white women did "apologize" for accepting the job and promised to rid the company of overt racism as soon as she could "settle in." Ten years passed with her still settling in, hiring and promoting only white females and white males -- aside from one Denzel Washington look-a-like black man. Connect the dots.

According to the black women I've interviewed, this condition is pervasive, a widespread practice in the places where they work. It's this kind of situation that foments political anorexia in black women, and makes them want to cry, makes them want to holler, and keeps them awake and alert and above all leery of working with or joining a white "sisterhood." Carolyn M. Brown, Editor-at-large at *Black Enterprise*, wrote an article on white women's "White Lies" in the January-February 2008 issue of *Pink* magazine frankly raising the question: "Are white women doing their part to support their black sisters in the fight for gender parity in corporate America?" When a senior vice president and director of recruiting at Chase Manhattan's Global Banking Division noticed a high number of black women leaving because they weren't promoted, she broke down the staff by race and found that white women "topped out" at the vice presidential level, but couldn't get into the "C-suite," while the black women were bumping up against a ceiling at the clerical level. It was then that the executive took a leave of absence to research the matter and found that the same was true at other companies, that black women were "trapped in the middle" of a situation where white women are afforded many of the privileges as white males," the *Black Enterprise* editor wrote in *Pink*. Beneath the white males at the top is "a tacit competition that pits white women against black women, whose battles are not one and the same even though both groups are fighting for gender parity."

Apparently "many white women are shirking their responsibilities as "sisters" in the gender movement and too often forget to "honor the covenant between all women," the CEO of The League of Black Women,

Sandra Finley, was quoted as saying.   Instead, when black women complain to them white women are prone to look down their noses and opine, "Oh, gee, that could happen to anybody." White men for their part are said to see black women as clerks while looking at white women as "their wives, mothers, grandmothers, sisters, aunts, daughters, nieces and granddaughters." Likewise the white women secretly see black women as "the hired help" or the white women's support crew. What is more, the editors report that "allegations of skin color have increased by 232 per cent over the last 15 years," doubling twice over. Plus black women experience a "two punch double whammy," of race and gender but insist that such embarrassments as being mistaken for a parking attendant at some plush affair is more likely to happen to them because of their race than their gender. But try getting a white female coworker to acknowledge this.

Loretta Walker at Turner Broadcasting System told how "animated and passionate" black women are seen as "aggressive" if they don't get regarded as a "rap star." Black women consequently may be moved to seek safety in a tight-lipped silence during company deliberations, something that may stifle career advancement in the long run. When black women band together they are said to be "self-segregating" and are subtly and sometimes expressly encouraged to disperse and avoid *hiring* another black for fear of appearing race-conscious. Part of the solution, says Johnson & Johnson's diversity education manager, Denise Beckles, is for white women to remember that black women are also "outside the good ol' boys network."

Many black women say they prefer to work with white men rather than white women. Reasons given: the white man shows you who he is immediately. If he's a racist, you recognize it from the git go. White women talk sisterhood and greet and embrace you and do their dirt and hide their hand.

I've heard white females say: "well, all white women aren't like this." I agree. And "all black women aren't stupid."

At a national convention of a prominent black educational sorority on the East Coast, I noted that some white females had been invited to the black women's seminars. In one of them a white lady stood up and said: "I'm white. But I would like some honest answers." "Why," she asked, "do black women refuse my invitation to join some of the white female political organizations or come to our meetings?"

A black female panelist then seized the microphone and told of the exclusionary history of such organizations as National Organization for Women, saying that in the history of NOW there had been only one black president, and she resigned after publicly calling them racist. She said their agenda was focused only on white female priorities and ideologies. The few black females who were members of NOW during that time came forward with their comments. Their discussion focused on how NOW leadership, with a history of preferring only white presidents, could represent organizations that include both black and white women. The black women had serious questions and observations. Who will be President? Who will set the Agenda? Who will determine media reps?

On another level, the answer to the question of why black women find it difficult to work with white women is no more complex than why white males find it difficult to work with black men. White males, like white females must be in control of the organization. This has historical ramifications. It isn't comfortable working under those traditionally categorized as "inferior". Some black women expressed their apprehension that too many white women don't want to work with black women unless black women are in subordinate positions. This attitude goes all the way back to the plantation, on through the childhood and adult experiences of white women, and it hasn't gone unnoticed in the observations of black females too often relegated to the underclass or left hanging on the lower rung of the ladder. In most organizations of blacks and whites it seems the whites have learned that black people are caught up with titles that don't really mean anything. They give them titles that don't control the organization but sound big: vice-president (the vice anything), assistant treasurer, the assistant to the executive director (assistant anything), sergeant-at-arms, the Provost.

Experiences like these – when not acted upon – tend to provoke a kind of political anorexia in the mind of a black woman and blocks out self-serving notions of coalitions of black women with white women for white definitions of women's liberation. White women react to sexism; black women must deal with racism as well as a different kind of sexism, because she's black and woman in a dual position and is sensitive to the possibility, if not the probability or even inevitability of being used against her race by the women of the white race that would subordinate and oppress her, the black woman. Thus the black woman is prone to feel that she must respond more to racism as it affects her children, her spouse and extended family. However, the white women will routinely insist on defining the agenda and the tone of speakers and the speaking, let alone the nature of any and all collective action.

This explains a lot of the black woman's relentless skepticism and reluctance to join with women who have not experienced her double jeopardy, or identity conflict. In comparison to white women, black women operate on a compulsive vigil depicted in *Black Rage* by psychiatrists Price Cobb and William Grier as "a healthy cultural paranoia."

The question accordingly remains, why join with women who are married to, sleeping with, bearing children by, and supporting the white males they themselves have accused of being sexist and racist but cling to them in order to keep their own place in the sun. Why don't they leave the plush suburbs and come over to live with us in the hood, if they want us to help them elevate the battle against their white male sexist tyranny? Women who are descendants of slave masters and slave mistresses appear unable to appreciate or fully understand the forces that have infected and continue to infect so many black women with the viruses of sexual and political anorexia.

In the early days of the 2008 presidential election, the black candidate, Senator Barack Obama, swept the state of Iowa with an amazing and historic victory. Although Jesse Jackson had been impressive enough as a veteran black militant activist running for office almost a quarter of a century ago to cause the Democratic party leadership to complete the establishment of the "superdelegate" tier of powerbrokers that would threaten Barack Obama's candidacy, many black people believed at first that white people weren't ready for a black president of the United States. In this context, some chose the white female candidate, Hillary Clinton, wife of former President Bill Clinton, beloved by blacks as "the first black president" based on his saxophone playing and swagger. Members of the Congressional Black Caucus had already stood on a lawn in tears lined up to support Bill in his own time of trouble. So when Hillary got to trailing in the polls in New Hampshire after coming in third in Iowa, she finally broke out in tears on television and then gave the impression she was being abused by the male-dominated media, provoking her husband to come out in her defense and attack Barak Obama with veiled racial innuendo such as what "America is not ready for." Then one of Hillary Clinton's surrogates, former Vice-Presidential candidate Geraldine Ferraro, came up with the absurdity that Obama wouldn't have made it as far as he had as the candidate for president if he hadn't been black. This was an example of how the white woman does not see things the way the black woman sees them.

For every black mother with a black male child, there's stress and anxiety to confront the moment they leave the house: racism and rejection faced by themselves and their males. Mothers in the Jim Crow South not long ago had to caution their sons and husbands and hold their own breath for fear that their men might be lynched or jailed unfairly, or otherwise suffer the fatal wrath of white racism. Today there remains a gnawing fear of police brutality, nooses, search, seizure and confiscation of items often planted on black males. Attorney Alton Maddox informs us in the *New York Amsterdam News* that "15 States have passed shoot to kill legislation, with no questions asked ... aimed at black males." Maddox went on to assert and explain how "mentacide and genocide are the twin evils against black males with no relief in sight."

Black women themselves are compelled to continue to live, see, taste and smell racism, a plague that follows them on job interviews, causing them sometimes to weep and whisper to themselves: "what will they think when they see a black face walk in here?" Or shopping while black: "I got stopped in an upscale store like this two weeks ago because black women are not expected to have the money for this store." Walking while black: "everybody whispered when I stopped in the coffee shop – you know I'm one of only two blacks in the subdivision." Jogging while black: "I got surprise glances from white women; they were thinking I couldn't be serious about jogging; aren't most black women overweight?"

A black woman faces oppression all around her all the time, even in her home, if only indirectly; whether she's married or single, it's present there. But leaving aside her battles with her man as fallout and residue of racism and its consequences – that is, fueled by racism and the forces behind it -- a black woman can turn on the television set morning noon and night and see no woman looking like her as co-anchor, newsreader, or talking head; even when the discussion is focusing on a black issue; a black woman can go for days without seeing someone who represents or looks like her on any pedestal, on any place of importance, unless she's into situation comedies and Butterfly McQueen.

An informal Black Think Tank survey of black females, ranging in age from 18 to 34, asked why the lack of solidarity between the black and white female. The majority of the black women gave an answer just the opposite of what we're used to hearing. They said the white female is jealous of them. One sister was adamant in her charge of this jealousy dating back to the early part of the twentieth century, when white fathers, grandfathers and other seasoned white men told their sons "you are not a man until you've been with a black woman."

Other reasons for animosity included jealousy of the black woman's fuller lips, which now have cosmetic surgeons and dermatologists swamped with white women paying loads of dough for lip and butt injections often referred to as "Big Gorilla Booties." They're paying to get what society calls "ugly," unattractive in the natural or organic god-given beauty of the black woman's African heritage. The "envy" argument includes the use of sun tan salons and saturation with sun tan oils in a quest to capture some semblance of the black woman's natural melanin. Some black women find satisfaction and comfort in their struggle for "beauty and acceptance" in a biological advantage they believe is often confirmed by observations that the darker the skin the slower the aging process.

The black woman's enduring difficulty in working together with white women crops up at every level and walk of life and is a forceful factor in the political anorexia of the black woman. At one point during Faye Wattleton's reign as the first black president of Planned Parenthood, Richard Nixon had come to office and called for legislation on population control aimed primarily at black Americans and Third World nations. Many observers interpreted Nixon's plan as sugar-coated euphemism for imposing stringent birth control on the black and nonwhite poor, including such strategies as involuntary sterilization for any girl giving birth out of wedlock for a second time, mindless of the fact that black girls don't get poor because they're pregnant but get pregnant because they're poor, while the middle class girl has abortions and is surrounded by information from her educated mother and other women in the family with knowledge and ability to take care of unscheduled pregnancies and births. Even their peer groups, including boyfriends of a similar culture, are exposed to adults with attitudes and behavior born of upward social mobility.

White female eugenicists "forgot" to alert their "black sisters" to the real meaning of the population issue. Black female survival has never been a keenly shared agenda of the white female gender. Partly because the more educated the woman the lower the birthrate, the white female population had come to the point where the white race was failing to reproduce itself, while the black birth rate continued to soar in the poorer classes all over the world, here and elsewhere So that there was even talk of a "birth dearth" in the white race at the same time as white authorities were wailing about the high birthrate of the black poor and "under-developed" nations. White modern day eugenicists saw this nonwhite "population explosion" as a "powder keg" of potential social unrest. Many black women thought they saw a hidden message of the population control hype, remembering as they did such previous clamors as "Urban Renewal" (which turned out to be "Urban Removal" of entire black communities). Also, they noted that one of the population control ploys of

Nixon era advocates was to turn the nonwhite poor away from marriage and childbirth and from welfare to workfare while resorting to middle class women and looser immigration practices to compensate for a decline in mass cheap labor.

Thus it was that Faye Wattleton found herself caught between the middle of doing the right thing and risking alienation from her employer, teetering and towing the line between social policies adverse to the interests of the black poor, risking the label "Aunt Thomasina" by going along just to get along with the power structure. In any event, Faye Wattleton resigned from her lofty position as head of Planned Parenthood.

Multitudes of black women in Faye Wattleton's position have appeared more willing to compromise themselves to keep their positions. There is this need to be acceptable to the going status quo ideology while involuntarily alienating the best interest of their own people. Unfortunately she wasn't and still isn't alone. The issue isn't so much whether population control is good or bad; it's about who decides and defines what's good or bad. No group or race of people, let alone the oppressors of another race, should have the right to decide the content of the major books published by another race, let alone to control the quantity and quality of their births and deaths, their population.

A highly placed black woman frequently finds herself in a compromised position, caught in a tortuous predicament on the horns of the dilemma of being hired to serve the interests of others against the needs of her people, where the needs of her people and others are frequently rear-enders, and these are among the things that foment political anorexia in a black woman's heart.

Disagreeing some years ago with white social workers on the theory and practice of black population control, parental and children's rights, black social workers drew a line in the sand. Their ideological differences were not based simply on the existence of another social problem but to avoid the extinction of a race. Yet many black social workers grew hesitant to push an agenda they deemed best for black inner city children, though their stance was completely opposed to the white position on the rearing and education of black children. However, they went as far as openly and collectively opposing white adoption of black children.

Political anorexia is suffered by many organized black women's groups that shield themselves from standing firm under an umbrella provided by those without the group's best interest. Part of the problem then and now is the political blindness of the middle class intellectuals, taking their cues from white propaganda and backing white politicians in opposition to better black candidates and black interests.

The black woman is often caught in the clutches of a sexual and political conflict between others that has nothing to do with her as a black woman *per se*. A case in point was the fight some years ago between the white liberals and conservatives, Democrats and Republicans and the sexual harassment case of Anita Hill in the hearings of Supreme Court Justice Clarence Thomas. Accusations of sexual misconduct such as Clarence Thomas coming over to hang Anita's pictures up on her apartment wall and the fact that Anita Hill left a message for him after dark informing him that she was in town were among the things that flooded the media and consumed public discourse. The drama made "Desperate Housewives" pale in the sunlight with the story playing out daily on national television and garnering more ratings than "The Young and the Restless." *The National Enquirer* had to go into overdrive keeping buckets of ink and rolls of paper for their overworked printing machines, with white females overwhelmingly supporting Anita Hill. But where were the white females among Anita Hill's colleagues and administrators at the University of Oklahoma Law School when pressure came down on the school from the Oklahoma powers that be? When the handwriting of probable dismissal was on the wall, her white cohorts and instigators sought and received more prestigious and loftier academic placements elsewhere, while Anita Hill faded from the scene and – though a graduate of the Yale University Law School – had to settle for a position in "Women's Studies" and later appointments peripheral and subordinate to her academic and professional merits.

When a black female organization invited Attorney Hill to address the group, the president of the organization, known to take no prisoners, asked Anita why she wasn't featured on magazine covers or plastered all over newsstands? They also asked if she knew why the first, only, and last black president of NOW (National Organization for Women) was conspicuously absent from airbrushed covers on major magazines on news stands? The women in the room expressed the view that if Anita Hill been a white woman, let alone the national president of NOW, her face would have been pictured and flaunted all over major newspaper and magazine stands.

It is such feelings and experiences of prejudice and mistreatment in situations of public humiliation, undergirded by a real sense of powerlessness to combat it, that place black women at such high risk of political anorexia. The political anorexia in turn also affects the inability of the black woman and the white woman to work together.

When O.J. Simpson was on trial, many white women – some who had dated him and received lavish expensive gifts -- stopped speaking to their black female co-workers when the verdict was rendered and black women cheered. Black women weren't cheering for O.J. Simpson; they were cheering because a black wealthy person like white wealthy men and women have always done, whipped the Justice Department. People couldn't understand why eight black women would let him off. They weren't letting O.J. off, if they were doing anything other than acquitting him on the evidence, they were avenging their sons and husbands, their fathers, lovers and multitudes of black men falsely accused by white women historically and lynched by white men. There are also the black men who have suffered incarceration under the crack cocaine law and automatic sentencing under the Three Strikes Law, husbands and lovers who have been stopped on suspicion when walking or "driving while black." Then maybe they were simply refusing to look at another black person in the police eyes. It is often said in the black community that white people think all blacks look alike, so how can you trust their eye- witness identifications?

White female news anchors continue to allude to Simpson whenever a male or female murder occurs and the victim is white, or anytime they think some man is getting away with something, all through the trial the name of Simpson is repeated. White women also say – and not out of love for O.J. Simpson that we have juries in this country and when they are exonerated they are free. A lot of people hadn't heard of the idea of a civil suit on top of a criminal trial, because we were always taught you couldn't be tried twice for the same thing.

Race also divided women when the Kobe Bryant accusation of molestation was raging. Was this woman forced to go to his room? We were taught to believe our system of jurisprudence support the decision of the jury. Women were also divided by race when a black women who brought charges against Duke University's La Crosse team were supported by black female organizations and individuals. White female groups were conspicuously absent. Black women wondered why so many women on talk shows would condemn the woman as a prostitute. Let me remind you that it was white feminists groups that had been arguing the notion that just because a woman is a prostitute doesn't mean she can't be raped.

Look at the United States Senate; there are no black females represented there in this most powerful decision-making group in the United Sates. All the female senators are white. The question is raised at most black female conferences: have white women invited black women to strategize with them to elect any black females to the senate?   Black women will get the white female senator's attention when they overcome their political anorexia or they can overcome political anorexia when they confront white female senators. Black women are not asking for position of first lady. It's obvious that is still a white female domain.

The book, *How Women Can Beat Terrorism,* by Curt Weeden, "makes a persuasive case as to why women must be on the front lines in the battle against worldwide poverty and not pushed to the side because of cultural, religious or social pressures."   Pushed aside is unerringly what black women are feeling. The book focuses on women in this country and Europe working together to empower women in poor countries. Why aren't women working together in this country to empower sisters in the hood?   Poverty of black women in this country is not microscopic. Whatever happened to charity beginning at home?

These elitist oversights -- ignoring women in ghettoes, in projects and slums, women on welfare raising fatherless children – contribute more than we know, or care to acknowledge, to the black woman's political anorexia and her reluctance to coalesce with women who ignore the poverty of black women in this country.

Blacks in the South often preferred white Southern red necks over the liberal "we're all one" liars because they knew how to deal with the upfront individual.

White women weren't so up front in their feelings. Their true but hidden feelings are often cloaked in false or conspicuous acceptance, seen by some black women as "devious." Some have interpreted this behavior as a shy cover up for feelings of competition and superiority. These women have been football queens, beauty queens, and icons of beauty and often referred to as trophies. They are thought to be icons of femininity and are placed on the pedestals of motherhood and womanhood. mTheir men and some black men have defined the world's standards of beauty on the white woman with the black woman last on the totem pole

This impels many black women to give up on the need to feel desired and desirable to her man and fall into fits of sexual anorexia in her resentment of a system that rejects her blackness and escalates the advantage of the white woman in the quest for desirability, not to mention the occupational and career gains. But the bottom line is the black woman's complaint that whether it's politics, a political campaign, a community organization, a church organization, women studies, or whatnot, the white woman must be in charge.

Chapter 6

Can Black Women Ever Unite?

Looking back on everything black women have gone through -- and are still going through -- we can understand why somewhere every day they seem to discuss the question of unity. In blistering telephone confabs and through the grapevine, we constantly bemoan our lack of unity; by cell phone, home phone, the treadmill, the vestibule of the church, the airplane, house parties, at work, under hairdryers in beauty shops, in nail shops, sorority caucuses and soirees, super markets, and any and everywhere we happen to run into one another. In coffee klatches we trace our disunity to some of the most outlandish issues; married, single, never been married; as Aretha would ask, "who's zooming who." Remember, we are known to develop high blood pressure and ulcers over somebody's designer clothes, or cars or condominiums -- wanting to be and remain "the only black" face on the corporate plantation.

In the whirlwind of coffee klatches and girlfriend lunches, we quickly get caught up in the lives of other sistas to the neglect of our own. If we could, we'd have national rumor mogul consulting agencies. We have become scrutinizers and architects of the lives of other sistas, the underground diagnosticians and interpreters of one another's actions. We've elevated ourselves to the position of judge, jury and hangman of the sistas we believe to be outpacing us financially, romantically.

There is this sista I know who doesn't call herself a spiritual monitor, but she appropriately fits the mold. She has this thing about who does and does not go to church every Sunday and what they might be doing. In the case of sistas familiar with the scripture "where two or more are gathered in his name" -- and choose not to join the parishioners -- the rumor mogul will not hesitate to spread the word that "two or more" are indeed gathered and engaged in a Sunday morning orgy in her home. Whenever I address adult female groups, campus and community organizations, a constantly misunderstood complaint is our unhealthy competition, jealousy and game-playing, our need for one-upmanship and our need to be acknowledged as the first, only and last black woman to achieve prominence and public recognition.

Competition is healthy. It keeps the blood and adrenalin pumping. But too often we enter the ring with the wrong opponent. Black women aren't running corporations in any significant numbers. Why aren't we seriously competing with those who are running corporations instead of one another?

Black women aren't represented in the United States Senate. Where is our competition with women of other races who are senators? We vote for and return other women to office every year, but we don't do that for our own.

Count the black female mayors of major cities, the urban Meccas supposedly producing so much crime. Why aren't we competing with those running for mayoral positions since our children are accused of being major perpetrators?

When a sister throws her hat in the ring we join the media, "is she qualified, does she have any experience?," just as we did prior to the Iowa and New Hampshire caucuses in the 2008 presidential election. Did Bill Clinton, George Bush, John F. Kennedy, or Jimmy Carter have experience as president of a country before taking the oath? Did Hillary Clinton have experience as a senator before moving to New York and becoming a senator? What experience did the present female governors have before becoming governors of their states? They had no experience. Yet when a black woman runs for office, we throw up the experience issue, the e-word, in her face.

The mainstream white media unrelentingly throw so-called research, polls and figures in our faces daily on young black children's obesity and its ominous consequences. We wouldn't have cooked that kind of food if black women would ban together and start our own fast food chains in major cities where we live. Black women are historically known to turn out everything fast, including fast food, because we've always had a million things to do trying to keep the houses of white men and women in order. Why aren't we competing for franchises to change these diabetes introducing menus making other fast food chains compete with us and change their ways? Black women can cook with or without fat-back and still keep it tongue-licking good. Then all too often our judgment on whether a sister is competent or incompetent is measured by how much we like or dislike her.

One day I sat down and opened one of my weekly must-read black newspapers. My eyes caught a headline, "IF CONDI RICE IS INCOMPETENT AS SECRETARY OF STATE IT'S NOT WHY MOST FOLKS THINK," written by one of my favorite columnists, Deborah Mathis.

During the highly charged deaths and bombings between Israel and Hezbollah, there was talk that the mystique of Condoleezza Rice was over. Why the sister was labeled a "mystique" remains a mystery to me. You might call her an anomaly but why "mystique?" According to Deborah Mathis, the television Republican talking heads -- many democrats as well as numerous black folk -- "began whispering that secretary of State was in over her head in dealing with the sticky, maddening, always impetuous Middle East. Some even tossed around the "I" word, also known as incompetence." No doubt the "N" word was served up with suburban dinner cocktails.

The columnist herself admits she never thought Condi Rice deserved to be Secretary of State, though she also never questioned Ms Rice's credentials. We've all read them. She has blurbs, resume and portfolios that her boss, the President, hasn't and never will possess. I wish to go on record for never defending Secretary Rice for forgetting her childhood Alabama roots and the racist slaughtering of her peers in the bombing of the church and three little black girls in the church in Birmingham, the hometown of Condoleeza Rice. I still don't approve of her ideology. Columnist Mathis argued "what makes her unfit as Secretary of State is not that she doesn't know what to do to make things better for global relationships, but rather that she doesn't do it. The man who gave her the job prefers diplomacy and lording over listening. It's his way or the highway, and Condi Rice is his parrot." "Rice," again continues Ms. Mathis, "has to know about feeling neglected, marginalized, unwanted, excluded, and punished for being an 'other.'"

If Ms. Rice has to bow, scrape and shuffle to keep her job, grinning and apple-polishing and go along to get along, this can be said of perhaps the majority of black women trying to climb the socioeconomic ladder and keep their jobs in the face of racist neglect, marginalization and exclusion for being an "other" commonly known as black? Are we incompetent because we allow ourselves to be judged by others who are riddled with racism, idiocy and stupidity?

Too many black women in high positions can, but will not, influence change. Like Condoleezza, other black women may be very active in politics in their own way but nevertheless fall victim to the condition of political anorexia (a loss of appetite for engaging in politics, particularly for the nourishment of self, in spite of the fact that you are surrounded by political festivities that invade our minds and bodies while a little voice keeps whispering to us : "if you speak up on behalf of black folk, you're going to be fired and out on the streets."

The implication is Condoleezza goes along just to get along. Can we cast the first stone or even the last one? Are we in a position to cast aspersions? When you say I can't get involved because of my mortgage note, my daughter's tuition, my new car payments, the Neiman Marcus annual "Last Call," you are going along with everything thrown at you in order to get what you think you want but not what you really need -- freedom. Can we criticize other sisters for scratching their heads and shuffling on the job?

Could our political anorexia be eating us up because we have the same fears as Ms Rice? We're simply playing on a different stage, with different footlights and a different orchestra. The music and the drama are the same.

One sunny afternoon in the uppity black section of the Oakland (California) hills -- with national and local elections only months away -- a prominent civic-minded sista held an impressive garden party for about seventy-five women to get together for fun and relaxation and catching up on the latest social and political happenings. When the city's only black elected female joined the party, she found the other sistas fuming. It appeared that the elected sista had an acute case of political anorexia, for in both her terms as representative of a black district and the only black elected female in the city, she had refused to hire black staffers, so that scorn and blasphemy were heaped upon her. Her white counterparts had mostly white staffers who looked like them (with a sprinkling of blacks for "multicultural" purposes), she was berated for not hiring blacks. Whether white, Gay, Jewish, Italian, Greek, Asian or Hispanic, other ethnics seemed to employ people for the most part who look like them, peppered only with individuals from other nationalities. When the sisters drilled the black elected official as to why no black people, especially black women, worked in her office, she said she was the black woman in the office and besides she wanted to show the public that she could be diverse in her hiring; she said hiring blacks would make her appear racist. Her problem was refusing to include black folk under the "diverse" label.

Competitors running for her seat included a black mother who had pulled herself and her children up from welfare, sent them to college and diligently pursued a degree herself while also keeping her community activism alive. When she hit the campaign circuit, one Black Anglo Saxon woman shrieked "oh we can't have someone who was once on welfare in an elected position. What better message can there be than to let the kids know that welfare, incarceration, slipping through the cracks doesn't have to be a death sentence; it could be the most powerful motivational force to keep them out of prison. Our government has almost every country, except Africa on some form of welfare. Does charity still begin at home?

I once sat in on a parent teacher conference concerning a young half Mexican half black boy who was in 6th grade and came home smitten with a little black girl. His black maternal grandmother backed the boy's half-Mexican mother's objections to his dating a black girl. This particular girl was an academic quiz kid, had magna cum laude grades in all subjects, and was facing a summa cum laude future at an Ivy League College. All she needed now was a scholarship to ensure her entrance to the City's top prep school. The boy's guardians had neither concern nor interest in the little black girl's present or future academic pursuits. Her intellect was immaterial. They objected to the girl's dark skin and braids. When asked why the concern with the young intellect's appearance, the mother and the grandmother asserted that dark-skinned girls with braids are products of the ghetto, housing projects, shelters and Section 8 Housing. Whoopi Goldberg could turn this script into a comedic tragedy.

One of my neighbors, a dynamic sister, was refused acceptance by several black social organizations due to her darker hue, which prompted her to say she suffered more skin color racism from blacks than she did from whites. This raised a haunting question: "Does self-inflicted racism exist among blacks as it does between the races? Racism is the use of power to deprive somebody of life chances - jobs, promotions, scholarships, access to health, admission to organizations and whatever the person seeks for mental, spiritual, economic and social gratification. When black people have the power to divest other blacks of these privileges, they're known as straw bosses and some are called Affirmative Action Negroes. Not necessarily synonymous to Affirmative Action Officers. Affirmative Action Negroes often act on behalf of their employer or someone over them. For instance, straw bosses are frequently used to administer racist test to keep out their own people. They are brought in by companies to perform hatchet jobs, mostly on their own people.

This serves more than one function. Hiring a black person to commit a racist crime keeps the company from being sued for racism. They are known to say we left the hiring to the Affirmative Action Officer who just happens to be black. These corporate flunkies practice the politics of the company and their hatred of self and the people who look like them. When these black folk sit on foundation boards established to fund community programs, the black representative seldom speaks up for programs in the 'hood.'

Some black agents for change can't be bought. When Janet Greene, an efficiency expert was called to reorganize positions in a major corporation, sisters in her Southern California circle wondered how she managed to get this awesome assignment. When I met her at a black women's conference in Los Angeles, I asked her point blank how she managed to do all these things and not be known as the most hated or envied black woman in the company. She said, since you have the courage to ask, I have the courage to answer.

She remembered some years ago perusing Niccolo Machiavelli's, THE PRINCE. When she was a sophomore in college and wanted to write a review of the book for a class assignment, the professor thought THE PRINCE outdated. He mocked the title. After all, who needed rulers and czars?

She nevertheless perused the book and stumbled upon a chapter entitled, "That We Must Avoid Being Despised and Hated." The book taught her that while some people are going to dislike anything you do, as they did with Jesus Christ, one has to be careful not to push the envelope too far. You can catch flies with honey easier than with vinegar. She said she always practiced avoidance of being despised in order to get things done, but strives to remember that integrity should never be sacrificed for the sake of winning approval and acceptance and accolades.

Sister Janet Greene also had a proclivity for holding up under pressure. She was once offered a high six-figured salary if she would accept the position of Minority Affairs Director for a major Eastern Corporation. On the day of the interview, the CEO welcomed her with much fanfare. He explained why the company had to lay off a major portion of its employees and why he felt it fair and equitable to lay off the last hired. You're familiar with the similarities in appearance of the last hired and first fired. Nothing mentioned about lay-offs according to competency, contributions to the company, loyalties or other humanitarian issues. The sister had to raise these questions.

The white CEO's answers, as you might expect, were evasive and replete with buzz words as in "cultural diversity", ethnic this or that and the usual jargon surrounding a company's "potential to protect itself." Cutting to the chase, the CEO wanted a hatchet woman to get rid of mostly black employees.

She thought longingly about what the sizeable salary could provide -- college educations for her children, home expansion, airline junkets to all the exotic company locales – and of course, there was also the temptation to bolster her frequent flyer miles. She was also divorced and the thought of meeting men in high positions with fat salaries did not escape her fantasies. She went home to think about the offer, promising to get back to the CEO within the week. That very same evening, she started making phone calls. She knew, notwithstanding the tempting salary, that she would not be able to live in that kind of comfort zone at the expense of other brothers and especially single sisters trying to make it on minimal salaries but the story doesn't end here.

She immediately got involved with the company's targeted casualties. Luckily she had a friend who had a friend working for the company. The friend arranged for the two to meet in the privacy of her choice – home, hotel or restaurant. These seasoned comrades knew the perils of black people noticed whispering or holding a private conversation about anything in a predominantly white work environment. Whenever two or more blacks are gathered laughing and chatting, some white onlookers will fear that some conspiracy or insurrection is about to explode.

When the invited black employees who could be trusted met at a hotel on the outskirts of town where the boss would never be caught taking his wife to dinner and valet parking was unheard of, they settled into a modest suite where they soon learned of the plot to eliminate their jobs. Janet Greene explained the companies intentions to pink slip the already lowest paid. They launched a winning plan of action, kept their jobs and in many cases, got promoted. The Strength Of The Lion Is Truly In The Pack!!

Political anorexia will not cure itself. A black male in a Southern city who was known for speaking up for the black community as well as feeding sick sisters and the elderly, sending black kids to college, and forcing the city to train and hire black males, was eventually sent to prison himself for not backing down on a position he had taken in some hot political issues involving several high profile politicians who had managed through financial and political connections to escape incarceration and remain in office and at home with their families. When the brother who took the rap was released from prison and sought to return to prominence in the black community, many black female political anorexics fell in line with the conventional wisdom that a black man like him shouldn't occupy a high position, because a man who had been to prison would set a bad example for the black boys. Although there may be some truth to this, there is also the undeniable fact that it is possible to come out of prison and lead a life for the good of the community. For instance, Malcolm X, who had not finished high school before entering prison, still managed to educate himself while incarcerated and upon his release was able to impact the race and gain worldwide respect for his role as a leader.

Maulana Karenga gave us Kwanza before going to prison, but it didn't really catch on and escalate until he came out; that's when Kwanza came into its own as a national black holiday celebrated by millions all over the world almost on a par with Christmas. After her release from prison, Angela Davis became a tenured University of California professor and continues to keep up her endeavors to reform prisons. Not to mention Don King, who served two prison terms for manslaughter before he became what many regard as the greatest boxing promoter of all time, bar none.

Former Black Panthers bounce from Princeton to Harvard and back to Princeton, at least one is the U.S. Congress, and two former members of the violent 1960s white Weather Underground movement are teaching at major universities in the Midwest.

Marion Barry, while mayor of the nation's capitol was entrapped before our very eyes on national television, then went to jail for six months before coming out and being elected mayor of the District of Columbia again. Even now, as I write, he is on the City Council. When a discussion on national and local black elected officials came up at a Washington, D.C. luncheon, the native Washingtonians were unanimous in their belief that if The Honorable Marion Berry, victim of police drug entrapment, who remains the most popular elected official in Washington D.C. ran for anything, he would win hands down over and over again. He keeps black businesses flourishing, black schools open and black folk working.

I once conducted seminars for some "lettered" black women who wanted to make a difference in a Southern city packed with low income housing projects, shacks, and infestation from germs created by outdoor toilets and other ecological problems. By now, we all know the drill and supporting anecdotes: "The Lord Helps Those Who Help Themselves." "Teach underserved people how to fish and they'll find their own pond."

"To be successful, you must involve those you deign to help." These affirmations may be a start but they aren't enough. After scouting churches, neighborhoods, and community activists stomping for equality, my assistants and I were able to come up with names of women who would make a considerable contribution on the road to putting the sexual and political anorexic demons behind them. We knowingly chose sisters who didn't live in the tony sections of town like the women in the social club set. The sistas we chose were living in squalor and experienced many of the conditions that concern us here. When we told the upscale women about the backbone of the sisters working with us, a lot of them fell to "hating on" other this or that sister. Questions flew: "Where does she live?" "Is she in the projects?" "Does she have a house full of children without a baby daddy? Is she on food stamps?"

The questions went on: Is she in public housing? Of course, the Black Think Tank staff chose women who lived in public housing. This organization of refined sisters never missed an opportunity to vote for President of the United States. I had to remind them that all presidents have and are presently living in public housing, the White House. You're paying their taxes; they're living free, so there you are. We put these multi-billionaires up in public housing and scorn our own sisters who time and again are deserted by their lovers, husbands, live-ins or otherwise visited by bad luck. This same organization caught flack for inviting the Secretary of State, who also was living in public housing tax free like the President, to keynote their anniversary celebration. In the end, she was a no-show.

Black women as a whole do not trust the integrity or expertise of each other. If we want something done and know there's a sister in our midst who is acclaimed at whatever the chore might be, we will go and seek some individual from some other race or ethnicity because we still believe their ice is colder than ours. We make such excuses as "oh she'll never get it done on time" or "black folk charge more than white folk." We think we're getting a better deal, better quality, and more publicity if someone who doesn't look like us is given the assignment. We buy from people that we accuse of selling us stale lettuce and meat in corner stores and super markets and perennial patronize stores neither hire nor look like us. And usually have individuals in the store walking around to see if we are going to steal some item while we are giving them our money.

Dr. Marva Collins, a former public school teacher who founded Westside Preparatory School in Chicago in 1975, is nationally and internationally known for her approach to teaching black children that public schools have failed. Her approach includes strong emphasis on the etymology and understanding of words, pronunciation, enunciation, classical literature, mastery of self and self reliance. Dr. Collins was nominated by four presidents of the United States to serve as Secretary of Education. She declined in favor of supervising her own school. She knew intuitively that if she accepted such a position, she would not be calling the shots. No matter how high profile an appointment may seem, you still have a master. Whenever you have a master, the master sets the agenda. Dr. Collins also turned down financial sponsors for her school (now schools) because of the adage: "he who has the gold makes the rules." She has been the subject of the CBS Award winning "60 Minutes Show" and a feature-length motion picture, "The Marva Collins Story," with Cicely Tyson cast in the role of Marva Collins. People from high level organizations, government officials and affluent private citizens seek her training for their schools and individual children from all over the world.

I first met Marva in Florida when we were guests on Tavis Smiley's "State of the Black Family," which was broadcast live on C-Span. Some months later we came up with the idea to engage twenty-five or thirty black women in a black female unity retreat in Hilton Head, South

Carolina. We put together a list of sistas representative of all black women who share a commonality in today's stresses confronting married and single black women on a daily basis. The women included journalists, media personalities, professors, house wives, married and single women, wives of corporate males, public and private school educators, university professors, attorneys, ministers, mental health practitioners and black women trapped in straight jackets of poverty. The letter of invitation explained why the legendary maverick, internationally renowned educator Marva Collins and I had decided it was time for black women to roll up their sleeves and make an indelible contribution to the black community and the world. We told the invitees they had been selected because they were individually talented and aggressive go-getters and light years ahead as a result of the many hats we as black women historically had to wear for the survival of our families, communities, and educational institutions. Because of what we collectively had to offer, we planned the retreat to address why so many spirited, cultural, learned sisters live "lives of quiet desperation," and why they are caught in a web of despair, apathy, and political and sexual anorexia.

Our goal was to bring our collective wisdom and experiences together and build a platform for swift and viable results we thought would surely emerge to modify and transform this unfortunate impasse into victory and triumph. We had black orators and lecturers in the group. All, but one had white agents making a mint off black speakers. During Black History Month, these agencies probably paid all their mortgages and bought new homes from the money earned from these talented black women. Our purpose was to establish our own agencies. Pool our resources to change the political landscape of black women in every discipline where other women were receiving the king's share of the pie. This approach of self-determination would be used in every employment and political issue involving black women. We would discuss relationships with black men and how to stop the bickering and misplaced rage that triggers sexual and political anorexia.

Just when we thought the juices were up and running, the old keep-us-apart envy, jealousy, and distrust began to surface. "Who's going to be President?" The letter had never mentioned a president. "Who will be in charge of the money?" We never ask that question in church. "Who will represent us and get their names in print and faces on camera?"

Would to thee that questions such as these would be posed to black leaders. Some of the sisters wanted to know: Who is going to be the biggest HNIC in the organization? And what are my chances of becoming the unspoken leader of the group? The questions were just flying in. Is anyone already widely known enough in this unity group that the public might identify as "their organization?" Will working for unity with this group offer any opposition or competition to my other organizations such as my sorority, my chances of making it into high society, or conflict with my husband's organization? What if a sister belonging to a different Greek organization than mine becomes the chairman? Will this be used as a recruiting device to the Chair's sorority? Is there anybody in the organization I've had a disagreement or falling out with in the past on any personal matter, especially over a man? How many single women in the group might be looking at my man or mate at one of our gatherings? How many "ho's" are in the group? Who's the best and most expensive dresser? Who has the biggest house? As a result, the meeting for black female unity never took place.

The critical point is here was an opportunity for black women to unite financially, emotionally and industrially through a method proven to be successful for Asian, Jewish and white women- - women who are more successful than black women because they unite for their shared elevation and thus have someone to watch their backs instead of their material acquisitions. If we want an excellent job done, we would rather get someone of another nationality we don't know than a competent sister whose work we're familiar with. The wise saying "familiarity breeds contempt" includes how it also breeds melancholic apathy, hopelessness, and political anorexia.

This quality of political anorexia is widespread and raging. You often hear some sisters saying, "Child, I wouldn't want to live in one of them big cities like Chicago or LA, 'cause it's entirely too much gossip going on and too much contention over which organization will accept you and which will not, and what is the class structure." While this may be notably present in such places as New Orleans and Atlanta, it is a frame of mind, this search for pedigrees that prevails in every village and every town, and it's present everywhere black women live. In Atlanta, a black female activist who was one of the city's top fundraisers and a strategic maker of politicians, indeed one of the top volunteers for philanthropic organizations anywhere, announced her retirement. At her retirement bash the invitees included politicians, political and social organizations, both high profile and grassroots groups and ministers who were recipients of her expertise and tireless service. The chief recipients of her generosity and charity included local, state and federal civil servants and politicians. One of the women joining the roast was struck by the conspicuous absence of politicians, most noticeably those who wouldn't have made it to the bathroom without her perseverance, persistence and determination.

A few of her black female "friends" present were pleased that so many major politicians and social butterflies were no-shows. They hurried to the ladies room to gather and participate in whispers, innuendoes and gossip that was continued at tables, restrooms and elevators. After all, who did she think she was? She wasn't a member of a silk stocking bourgeoise church; Greek-letter female organizations had shunned her quest for membership. In her youth, she allegedly dated men from the cradle to the grave. The tittle-tattle continued far into the night only to be resumed the following day on telephones and emails.

The repulsion and absence of major black parasitic politicians noted by both black and white guests hardly equaled the actions of some black female heads of organizations and political wheeler dealers. These black female political gatekeepers came to the rescue of the black male politician known never to date black women – but blamed the victim, the sister, the honoree, for the actions of such grossly unappreciative and absent politicians. The gossipmongers asked each other why the honoree would expect the political nobility to come to honor someone who is not considered "A" list, especially the most noticeable absentee, the black politician she did the most for.

How can black women ever unite with this raging sister-to-sister envy? Political and sexual anorexia have killed many female relationships. We've allowed it to block our socioeconomic progress, our political liberation and our romantic relationships, so that now our sisterhood is locked in a self-destruction mode.

One instance comes to mind in a city that shall remain anonymous but is able to boast of several theme-based museums and unusual attractions and interests for both national and intercontinental collectors, one of them the new Asian Museum made possible by Asians in high places working with black officials including a black female who was on the board that bestowed this bonanza upon the Asian community. Good for them! The Asian Museum was born when the city's new main library was being rebuilt. The old library was housed in a magnificent building with an antique esthetic people would come from all over the world just to look at it. But history was giving way to technology, so the city planners got the idea to build a new high-tech computerized library, leaving the historical architectural masterpiece up for grabs, while the black community was kept in the dark. After the library's acquisition as an Asian Museum came to light, the black community met and asked the black female city council woman, who had been placed in office by a black district, why the black community had been kept in the dark when the building was put up for potential bidders. The black elected official cocked her head and arrogantly replied that the black female activists and artists should have asked, like the Asians did, if they wanted the building. She was asked how black folk would have known the building was up for acquisition if nobody told them and it wasn't advertised in public places. The black elected official, repeating her dictum that "the Asians asked for it," added the insult that "they (Asians) probably know how to run a museum." "What experience have blacks had with such an artistic endeavor?" she quipped.

Never mind that this political and artistic neophyte had no known experience or prior record as an elected representative until black women went out and pushed door bells in housing projects, selling fried fish, chicken dinners and sweet potato pies to finance her campaign. Why didn't she tell the black community the building was available? It came as no surprise when news got out that the Asian councilwoman had informed her constituents of the possibility of occupancy of the landmark edifice. But chickens really do come home to roost. When this sister lost her seat as an elected official in the very next go-round, her position went to an Asian female.

My, my -- God is good!

The museum story doesn't end there. Blacks, with the instigation of outside sources were offered an opportunity to build a black museum, but nothing that would compare in its edifice or its ambience with the cathedral quality of the Asian museum.

As for the new black museum, the powers-that-be appointed a board of directors that would change its membership (including the director) as often as you change your underwear. The board was asked to locate a person with museum expertise as its first director. The bourgeois sisters on the museum board launched an expensive national search, replete with white headhunters bouncing around the globe on "visits" and "consultations" with museums in foreign lands. They eventually brought in a black woman from elsewhere (who had "done some work in Europe"), overlooking a multitude of qualified local black women with museum experience right in the city where the museum was to open.

Following a burst of community pressure, a merry-go-round of different sisters were brought in and subsequently banished, amid rumors of ineptitude, lack of experience and the absence of a simple acquaintance with the inside of a museum, let alone its inner workings. This includes the last one who was dumped The only black museum in town has now hired a white female , with no curatorial museum experience, as the new director of a black museum, charged with bringing in black artifacts from Africa and the Diaspora. As of this writing, the museum remains in a multicultural mess, and it is rumored that it probably is going to close.

This is one of the many reasons black women may never unite, or makes it so hard for us to work with and work for our people. Of all the black women in town they went somewhere else to find a museum director, not respecting competent candidates among us, so the organizers wound up with a white woman who has never directed a black museum.

Then they even brought in a black man trailed by his white wife from the Ivy League as a "consultant" to explain the meaning of such as "the Diaspora" at the tune of one million dollars, according to the buzz. It doesn't get any worse than that.

This kind of back-stabbing envy and resentment of other sisters didn't happen so much with our ancestors, grandmothers, or mothers. They clung together for their survival, family, community and even neighbors and extended family. Only a few weeks ago a sister in the District of Columbia was reminiscing with me about the 'good ole days' when black women were eager to compliment each other. If they saw someone in the church with a great hat: "Oh Miss Jones, where did you get that fabulous hat?"

Miss Jones not only told you where it came from, she bragged about getting it for nickels and dimes instead of pricing it out of the inquiring sister's reach. When Miss Jones baked pastries for a church event, the cake was always "screaming!" Women couldn't contain themselves. They would ask out right, "Did you really bake it?" Miss Jones would grab her hand and say "come on back here honey; I made two cakes; cut this one in half and take some home for your children and husband."

A prominent black female pastor and theologian, comparing today and yesterday, told me how these things have changed between black women. "Today's heifers would never comment or compliment the hat, nor the cake." The outraged cleric went on to report that we now prefer to "go behind your back to say the hat was 'hot off the streets,' the corner store man gave you the ingredients for the cake for sleeping with him."

Shrinks and the mental health community attribute much of this pent up venom to the many worries confronting sisters today.

Political and sexual Anorexia continues to fester at the core of much of this. Jane and Robert Handly, in *Why Women Worry and How to Stop*, organized a focus group to see how the women follow a psychosocial path to worry. Despite the consequences of childhood, whether privileged or poverty-ridden, many women had slipped into low self-esteem. The Handlys found financial concerns were the most common reason. Most of their other concerns centered on their intimate relationships, body image and appearance.

Relationships: "Finding someone who will love me," "losing my boyfriend or husband," 'being alone."

Personal appearance: "Being too fat,' "too skinny," "having a bad complexion."

Pleasing (or not pleasing) others.

"How to be assertive without losing my femininity," "how to say no to requests without offending others"

Making the wrong decision. "problems with my marriage." "questions about my career," "What if I never get married?" Growing old, "Wrinkles"

Clearly women are worried about their appearances, being too fat, too skinny, having a bad complexion, pleasing or not pleasing others, being assertive without losing their femininity, and attracting and holding a mate.

I once spoke to a group of 500 black business women. Some owned their own businesses. Most were college graduates from prestigious institutions, and some had climbed the ladder to top managerial jobs. During the coffee and networking break, the staff circulated forms raising the question: "What Makes/Would Make You as Happy, or More Happy than Your Present Position?" Later their feelings were compiled and evaluated. In first place, without a close second, was "finding a man or someone to love me." These women had "made" it in the work place "only to discover," in the words of Christopher Lasch in *The Culture of Narcissism,* "that emancipation from (all ancient taboos) brings neither sexual nor spiritual peace."

Some of the most divisive sistas appear to be poised to exploit each and every possibility for division they can devise. This can be something as picayunish as whether they are married or single. The sexual anorexic woman is often single, but even when she is married, she is likely to be lonely and think differently than sistas who have escaped, at least for the moment, the avaricious clutches of sexual anorexia. When she's married, she fears the divorce her friends too frequently experience will happen to her and impact her two incomes, and feels she will not be able to bear the prospects of a situation in which she can no longer maintain, on one income, the lifestyle to which she has become accustomed. In the case of a single woman, her safety is always on her mind. She needs to live in sections of the city she considers safe. These areas are usually more expensive. Working late, driving alone and into an empty garage is unsettling with today's crime rates. A condominium or apartment building with a doorman does not totally set her mind at ease. The doorman, among others, knows her schedule and her comings and goings schedules. This often keeps her closed inside of the apartment and into herself. She is reluctant to invite the men she does meet into her place.

The married woman also has her share of political and sexual anorexia. It doesn't usually take years of marriage before she notes things aren't going according to soap opera expectations. Some of her single friends will often appear to be doing better materially, especially the ones with money and achievement. This often makes the married woman resent sharing what she has with husband and family. It often leads to dishonesty where joint ventures, checking accounts and savings are involved.

We still have those sisters who buy clothing, rush home before husband and hide their goodies in the closet. Sometimes when a married sister wears her new pieces and her mate admires or asks when did she get the shoes, where did you get the suit, she replies a little sheepishly, "oh I've been having these for years." She wonders if she would have owed anybody an explanation if she'd been single. It seems the grass is always greener on the other side of the fence.

The married sister may think that every day is a party for her single friends, while the single woman envies a married woman's presumption of constant companionship, not recognizing that a lot of married brothers are working odd jobs or odd hours, split shifts, and may be involved in other diversions that take them out of the home and into the streets. The single woman sees the married woman as lying in her luxurious bed with a good-looking man next to her, while she in fact must spend her nights surrounded only by a pile of romance novels and sexual toys.

The unattached woman will often seek out someone to accompany her to social events. She doesn't need this anymore, but her old fashioned upbringing has convinced her to always "go" with a man.

In the absence of a male in her life and voluntary or enforced celibacy (sometime brought on by the man she chose or the path she has experienced), she may be impelled to overcompensate in unnecessary expenditures on hey-look-at-me-and-come-get-me clothes in her search for gratification. She may take on an appearance of nymphomania in a desperate attempt to get back at the men who lied to her, disappointed her, broke pledges of monogamy or were seen to be promiscuous by her family and friends.

Though there really is no shortage of men for sexual encounters, the sexual anorexic, having lost her appetite for the war between the sexes, too often finds difficulty in stomaching the men she meets. In this condition she becomes aggrieved and disdainful of going out on dates. Meanwhile, when the single woman gets with her married friends, she will boast of her independence and often alienate the married woman when the opportunity presents itself. By contrast, the single woman may resent the married woman because the married woman enjoys the benefits of two salaries or incomes while the single woman may feel doubly disadvantaged and dispossessed because she has to live on one salary without the help of a man, although in many instances the single woman may have an income larger than the married woman and her husband put together.

Now the competition moves to another level. The woman not experiencing sexual anorexia may boast of the man she has while the anorexic sister may boasts of the material goods she has amassed and they alienate each other in a sadistic cycle of competition.

An acquaintance of mine, a childhood friend who is now a full adult, was experiencing sexual anorexia because of her repetitive disappointment in multiple relationships with single *and* married men, and anything else she could find. Out of her disappointment, she resorted to an endless refrain of justifying her own situation; it seemed she was forever extolling her virtues, singing her own praises, fantasizing, inventing, concocting, and pathologically lying about imaginary men and relationships.

Today, the black male shortage exacerbates the pain of sexual and political anorexia and is a huge contributor to black female disunity and discord, as the surplus of males flitter from one female to another without making and keeping a commitment. When a man bounces from one woman to another, he foments discord, because he dashes the hopes of the woman he left behind as well as her confidence in other men. Of course the same is true when a woman breaks her commitment, she contributes to the sexual anorexic virus later carried by the man. Dating husbands and boyfriends of friends, extra-marital affairs, and bickering between single and married women, are things that have caused many black female organizations, notably Greek organizations, to inaugurate and uphold a "Moral Turpitude" clause forbidding any scurrying, scampering and scrambling for the other women's men . Translated: *"Thou shalt not date, sleep around with or be caught with another sister's man".* A Greek-lettered friend once tested this clause and went out and around with one of her soror's husbands. In return she received more than a slap on the wrist and has yet to recover; they did put her out but she wore a scarlet letter and every time she entered a meeting she could feel their eyes on her.

With all eyes on the black woman she must keep her eyes on the prize, while finding new and creative ways to sort out and see clearly what stands in the way of her happiness as a black woman and whatever it is that she wants. The black woman is poised to choose among her complicated but multiplying options for a new beginning. She must recapture the legacy of the millennia so impressively recorded by contemporary white archeologists certifying her preeminent place in the origins of the human race (confirmed and validated with the discovery of the fossil remains dubbed "Eve" in Africa). The black woman is "the mother of the universe." Not only that, throughout the recent centuries of our enslavement and oppression, the black woman has continued to be "the backbone of the black family," a sociological fact not lost on today's families of black women with children, where, for whatever reason, the presence of a male is the exception rather than the rule. We at the Black

Think Tank know and have said before that in a racist patriarchal society it is the black male who poses the primary threat to the white male oppressor, who in his mind can take his place in the bedroom and the boardroom. The oppressor knows that if the black male does not thrive the black family cannot thrive. As the late black novelist John O. Killens wrote in *And Then We Heard the Thunder*, "the last thing they want is for a black man to be a man."

Quite some years ago, when the Black Think Tank surveyed black men and women on their frustrations and feelings in male-female relationships we found that black males tended to concede that the black woman has been the backbone of the black family. We found that the black man secretly tends to look up to the black woman, but resents it. Black females also confessed that they were proud of their so-called "strengths," but the black female cannot be a woman (a full human being) and remain a slave any more than a black male can be a man. The black woman can play more of the functions of a man just as the black man is often relegated to play more of the role of a woman (which we have seen to be epitomized in the pimp (in the chapter on "The Black Male Carrier of the Virus of Sexual Anorexia). Nevertheless, the black women we talked to were proud of their strengths but feared these very strengths would someday be the death of them in their relationships with their man. Most said they would give their right arm to have a strong black man to stand behind them.

Today, according to the great Kenyan scholar, Ali Mazuri, the black woman has sold her birthright for a place in the corporations and companies (postmodern replicas of the Antebellum plantation) where the black women work and struggle in the status of a "minority" and they feel they must enter the workplace wearing a scarlet letter. The black woman walks into a fierce firestorm of stereotypes that are forever in place, however subtle and secretive. She learns that she is not expected to be anything but the Jezebels their white coworkers and "superiors" conceive her to be, their statue on the street, and black women are very aware of that conception. They frequently feel they are not regarded as worthy of high end department stores. It is thought they don't have the money -- you're in there to steal or do something dysfunctional. And even when the white female clerks come sweetly up to you with a saccharin greeting or stop you in the course of your shopping, they're sending out the impression to you, the black woman feels, as well as to onlookers that you as a black woman must be some kind of a thief.

Wherever we go, or wherever we socialize, the response to the black woman is felt to be the same. You're miseducated and pitifully obsessed with a crass but uninformed materialism you can ill afford, coveting clothes, cars, jewelry and shoes (they appear to think we all have a shoe fetish). They assume that none of us exercise. Even when we walk into the spa or the gym they stand and pause and wonder, you suspect, "what is this black woman of color coming in here for?" Oh, she'll probably use the treadmill or something, certainly not any of the complicated weights to tone her body. If you're overweight -- and the Center for Disease Control is constantly pumping out releases, it seems most every day, on the black woman's relative obesity, how overweight the black woman is compared, always, to the white woman.

Within the social fiber of the culture of friendship and individual relations, the black woman is not fully allowed to form friendships with other black women on the job, being just a little afraid to do that because it seems always to be thought that you must be discussing race issues or some insurrectionary black intent.

White society observes that we're not in high profile jobs, members of the U.S. Senate, top levels of major corporations and financial institutions, and conclude that we're not qualified, not ready on day one, don't have the experience we've been denied by a racist past and present. Thus you are relegated to an inferior rank and role or status (which translates into you're incompetent, you're inferior). Even when a black woman does get to a high profile position, it is typically thought: "She just slept her way there," or "I know how she got up to that position." The belief is you were too incompetent to get there any other way.

They think our children are bad because black women can't control them, because there's more crime and delinquent black youth shown on television, because of the motto of the media saying that if it bleeds it leads, and all the bleeding is thought to go on in the black community.

The only way black women are going to change our image is change it for ourselves – not only by, for, and to ourselves but also to society, and to do this it is necessary now, from this moment on, to become combat divas.

 This is not to suggest that we are going to spend all of our time avenging racism or getting back at those who oppress us, but we do have to begin to put a stop to these insults. We must stop letting other people speak for us and speak up for ourselves.

One of the most vital things that we don't have is a platform or the power of media outlets. We have to build them, build our own programs, knowing that nothing can make your life work for you if you're not the architect. The white dominated society and its diabolical talking heads and cunning opinion-makers have become the almost exclusive architects defining what black women are and can be, and we must put a stop to that.

We must have combat divas. Why not? We have hip hop divas, we have church choir divas, we have operatic divas, we have ghetto divas; yet we don't have combat divas. We are not prepared to do combat with our oppression by our enemies, neither within nor without. We must not overlook the enemy within. It is the role of the combat diva to protect not only herself but her people, the "crabs in the barrel." Consequently once we have combat divas, the first thing we must do is eradicate and stop the backbiting among ourselves.

We must have unity. Stop playing bridge and start building bridges, bridges across the rivers of our divide, bridges across the rivers of familial, racial and gender disconnect. Martin Luther King once reminded us if we ever had unity we'd get more freedom than the passage of a thousand laws. We must have unity of black women, unity of black women and black men, unity of a people, unity and self control. We must have control of ourselves.

First we must take back the control of our children, seize back our children's minds. Especially the boys, because that is one of the main reasons black women do not unite with one another, they're so busy fighting and bashing each other over the vanishing black males. The absence of the male in our lives is a source of the epidemic of sexual anorexia. We must rear the boys we wish our girls to marry. Train our boys as if they are going to marry one of our daughters. Someone once said that intense love is often akin to intense suffering -- and that's what you see happening out there, when we are in the throes of sexual and political anorexia.

If you know your daughter is going to marry one of the male carriers of sexual anorexia, this is the kind of thing, the kind of behavior we have to train our girls against. We must be as diligent in bringing the black girl to womanhood as we are in bringing the black boy to manhood. Help her to know what kind of mate to look for, to be comfortable in herself and bonded with the family and her family values, so that she will be less likely to depart from them. Teach her to be the value setter a woman must be. Sometimes this will be in contrast to what the white-dominated society may decree – running against their dictates of ultra-permissive childrearing; and this goes especially in the case of our training of the boys. We must tell the white oppressors that if they do not tell us how to rear our children we will not tell them how to rear theirs.

We must endeavor to expunge our families of the scourge of unattended and neglected latchkey children, organizing to meet and keep and teach the children until their mother returns or when their parents are not at home when their kids come home from school.

Find out what our children need, help them to know who they are and what they want to become, as well as what it is that stands or may stand in the way of it. We cannot stand by while our men and our children perish. Where were we in the so-called drug war, when drugs were being flown in from other countries to our communities to corrupt our young and our children, sometimes helping to launder or dispose of the cash or look the other way when they brought in all kinds of new clothes and everything money could buy? Where were we when they passed the racist crack cocaine laws where a person guilty of possessing crack (the cheap drug of choice for inner city blacks) received debilitating sentences while those with high priced cocaine, white and middle class, got off with a slap of the wrist. Where were we when they passed the "three strikes" law they knew would disproportionately devastate young black men. Do we understand that when they take away our males, they are taking away our husbands and our mates, our sons and our father?" Why do we stand by while the gangs overrun our communities and our children, our future. This is a blight on the black condition that will continue until somebody puts a stop to it; and we are the ones that must jump in and do that.

We must become combat divas. And once we become combat divas, there can be no issue that black women cannot get in there and speak on it. We can no longer leave this to the people who would oppress us and diminish our children. Our men are being depleted, as prisons become the new black plantation and unemployment among inner city youth becomes the norm.

Today, the black woman is fast becoming the only group that is left that can stop the new slavery and incarceration of black males. Just as it was necessary that we go into segregated schools, sometimes leading children by the hand (although at the behest of male-led post World War II civil rights organizations such as the NAACP). We must begin to step up to the podium, when there is a political issue going on and they are talking about "women and minorities." Demand that if they refer to the black woman and the black man and the white man by race, they should also call the white woman out by race, not just women presuming to represent all women. Black women have to stop believing that when they talk about women as a gender they are talking about black women too; when they say "women" we have to clarify whether they're including black women or just white women, because they are not the same, anymore than when they lounged and hid in the back of the house when we were slaves, mammies for their babies and concubines for their men, then later maids and housecleaners for their plush homes and mansions.

Like even right now, as I write these words, the television talking heads and opinion-makers keep saying "a black man and a woman" are running for office, when they know it is "a black man and a white woman." This leaves the black woman out. If they really want a black person or woman they would choose a black woman, and they would have both a black person and a woman. The choice would be easy, but they will cloud your vision and manipulate your minds as long as you allow it. This we know, for it has been something that has persisted through all the generations of our emancipation.

When we say nothing about misrepresentations when people are presuming to talk about us, we validate the issue that all the women are the same. If a television station says forty percent of our employees here are women, we have to ask how many of them are black. Never mind the buzzwords "multiculturalism" and "diversity" that replaced "affirmative action" (the balance of which, figures now show, got the most and reaped the whirlwind after the 1960s). Make them break it down by race, so we can see if they intend to get around to us. If you don't demand that they tell you how many will be black, you may be validating their secret wish to make you invisible.

And yet, a lot of us continue to believe that any progress, any major change, or any positive thing for black people will come from the racist system and the government. Racism speaks for itself, and the only time the government comes in is when they see you've started some serious activism or the threat or thought of resistance, that you are getting ready to do something about your situation. It is then when they will rush to jump in and control it. We must remember that the most potent and important weapon in the hands of the oppressor is the mind of the oppressed.

We must seize back our own minds and our households and families, and this demands that we become combat divas. Just as in the military, as combat divas dedicated to serve until the black woman and her children and family unit receive our rightful due. It is necessary that we constantly stay at attention, on guard and at attention, standing tall as combat divas.

Beneath the black female's persona, there is an endless longing, an unrequited craving, a never fulfilled desire: a perpetual begging to be valued, a begging to be respected, to be loved and elevated, just like the white female. How long must the black woman continue to ask, "Ain't I a woman?" How come I as a woman "ain't never been on no pedestal, on nothing beyond these high heel shoes."

We want our turn to be on the pedestal, up there in the higher echelons of life, on the pedestal of polite society, but we have never been there since our encounter with our enslavement. The late great tennis player, Arthur Ashe, was quoted once as saying: "Being a black man in America is like having another job." Well, being a black woman is like having two jobs, raising and caring for the children and caring and doing for the man, or if there isn't any man, you have to make ends meet alone, while everybody else has somebody else to help them. We've worked ourselves to death for others; now let us work for ourselves.

The time has come now: the time is now, when, having been through what we've been through, we can no longer let anyone demand more respect than the black woman. We are the mothers not only of the black race but the nursemaids of the founders of this nation. In fact, we can say with confidence and humility that we are the mothers of the universe. The oldest archeological findings confirm that now, the skeletal remains of the human being the white anthropologists dubbed "Eve" has been conceded to have been the first human being so far discovered on earth. If that is so, Sojourner spoke the truth to us almost two centuries ago when she said, "If the first woman God made was strong enough to turn the world upside down all alone, we ought to be able to turn it back and get it right side up again." If the first woman on earth could impact the world the way Eve did, all by herself, and as you know she was black, imagine what black women, now millions strong, millions of combat divas could do today.